Bible Summary

Every Chapter of Scripture in
140 Characters or Less

Chris Juby

Licensing can be discussed by emailing licensing@biblesummary.info.

ISBN 978-1533448552

This print-on-demand edition is published via CreateSpace.

The cover image is my great aunt's Bible, opened at Psalm 119.

Contents

Foreword

Have you ever had an idea that seemed daft and brilliant in about equal measure? That's how I felt when I first thought of summarising the Bible on Twitter.

It was July 2010. I was looking for a way to focus my daily Bible reading and I decided that writing a short summary of each chapter would help. Twitter was very much in vogue, and it struck me that if I kept the summaries under 140 characters I could publish each one as a single tweet.

I registered the @biblesummary account and spent a couple of weeks building a website. Then every day for three-and-a-half years I woke up, read a chapter of Scripture, studied the themes, and posted a summary to eventually 30,000 followers. It's no exaggeration to say that the project changed my life.

I summarised on birthdays and anniversaries, Christmases and New Year's Days, on excellent days, on horrible days, from hotel computers in France and Spain, from my mobile phone perched on the top of hills, and twice from the maternity ward.

The book in your hands is the end result.

Consider these my notes on each chapter, a kind of study aid for Scripture. I often refer to them myself when I'm looking for a Psalm, or trying to remember where a story appears.

I have tried to be as even-handed as possible, only reflecting what I found in the chapter. But of course much that is important has been lost in the reduction, and the summaries are certainly no substitute for the real thing.

Rather, my hope is that this book will inspire you to read and understand the Bible for yourself, and that through reading you will hear the eternal Word of God speaking afresh.

If you're interested in finding out more about the Bible Summary project you can follow the Twitter account at @biblesummary, or visit www.biblesummary.info for the blog and a full archive of the summaries

My deepest thanks go to Wes, who convinced me that there was a little more brilliance than daftness in the idea, and to Hannah, who believed in the project even when it cost us.

Chris Juby, Durham
May 2016

Genesis

1. God created the heavens, the earth and everything that lives. He made humankind in his image, and gave them charge over the earth.

2. God formed a man and gave him the garden in Eden, except for the tree of knowledge. Adam was alone so God made a woman as his partner.

3. The serpent deceived the woman; she and Adam ate from the tree. The earth became cursed, and God sent Adam and Eve out of the garden.

4. Eve's sons made offerings to God. Only Abel's was acceptable, so Cain killed him. Abel's blood cried out and God sent Cain away.

5. Adam's line was: Seth, Enosh, Kenan, Mahalalel, Jared, Enoch, Methuselah, Lamech and Noah. Noah's sons were Shem, Ham and Japheth.

6. Humankind corrupted the earth with evil. God decided to destroy them. He told Noah to build an ark to be saved from the flood.

7. Noah and his family went into the ark with two of each creature. It rained for forty days and forty nights and the earth was covered.

8. The flood abated. Noah sent out a raven and two doves. When the earth was dry God called them all out of the ark. Noah built an altar.

9. God blessed Noah and set the rainbow as a sign that he would never flood the earth again. Noah got drunk and cursed Ham's son Canaan.

10. Japheth's line lived in the coastlands; Ham's included Nimrod and the Canaanites; Shem's lived in the East. These formed the nations.

11. They began building a great tower for themselves, but the Lord confused their language. Shem's line included Abram who married Sarai.

12. God told Abram, "Go. I will make you a great nation. You will be a blessing." In Egypt Abram lied about Sarai and Pharaoh was cursed.

13. Abram journeyed with his nephew Lot. Their servants argued, so Lot went to Sodom, Abram to Canaan. The LORD promised Abram the land.

14. The kings went to war and took Lot captive. Abram rescued Lot. Melchizedek blessed Abram and Abram gave him a tenth of everything.

15. The Lord promised Abram an heir and many descendants. Abram believed. He was told that they would be enslaved but would then return.

16. Sarai told Abram to have children with Hagar. Hagar conceived, then ran away, but an angel sent her back. Hagar's son was Ishmael.

17. God made a covenant with Abram and renamed him Abraham. He renamed Sarai Sarah and promised them a son. The men were circumcised.

18. Three visitors came and said that Sarah would have a son next year. Sodom was very evil; Abraham pleaded with the LORD for the city.

19. Angels took Lot out of Sodom. The city was destroyed by fire and Lot's wife was turned to salt. His daughters had children for him.

20. In Gerar Abraham said, "Sarah is my sister." King Abimelech took her but God warned him in a dream. He restored Sarah to Abraham.

21. As promised, Sarah had a son: Isaac. She had Hagar and Ishmael sent away but God preserved them. Abraham and Abimelech made a treaty.

22. God told Abraham to sacrifice Isaac. As Abraham obeyed, an angel stopped him. The LORD provided a ram instead and blessed Abraham.

23. Sarah died in Kiriath-arba. Abraham asked the Hittites for a burial site. He bought a cave from Ephron and buried Sarah there.

24. Abraham's servant went to Nahor to find a wife for Isaac. He met Rebekah by the well. She went back with him and married Isaac.

25. Abraham died and was buried with Sarah. Isaac and Rebekah had twins: Esau and Jacob. Esau sold his birthright to Jacob for a meal.

26. In Gerar Isaac lied about Rebekah. He grew so rich that Abimelech sent him away. He dug wells, and at Beersheba the LORD blessed him.

27. Rebekah and Jacob tricked Isaac into giving Jacob his blessing. Esau vowed revenge so Rebekah told Jacob to go to her brother Laban.

28. Isaac sent Jacob to marry one of Laban's daughters. On the way Jacob dreamed of a ladder reaching to heaven and the LORD blessed him.

29. Jacob worked for Laban seven years to marry Rachel, but Laban gave him Leah and made him work seven more for Rachel. Leah had sons.

30. Rachel's maid had sons for Jacob, then Leah's maid, then Leah. Finally Rachel had a son. Laban allowed Jacob flocks as wages to stay.

31. The Lord told Jacob to return home. Jacob left in secret and Rachel took Laban's idols. Laban chased Jacob but they made a treaty.

32. Jacob heard that Esau was coming to meet him. He was afraid and sent gifts. That night he wrestled with a man who renamed him Israel.

33. Esau and his men arrived. Jacob bowed down but Esau ran to embrace him. Jacob settled near Shechem and built an altar.

34. Shechem raped Jacob's daughter and asked to marry her. Jacob's sons told him to circumcise his men, then Simeon and Levi killed them.

35. Jacob went to Bethel and God renamed him Israel. They journeyed on. Rachel died having Israel's twelfth son. Isaac died in Hebron.

36. Esau's sons were Eliphaz, Reuel, Jeush, Jalam and Korah. Esau and his family moved away to Seir. They became the Edomites.

37. Joseph was Israel's favourite son. He had dreams and his brothers were jealous so they sold him. He was bought by Potiphar in Egypt.

38. Judah's sons Er and Onan died, leaving Tamar a widow. Judah sent her away but she put on a veil and he slept with her. She had twins.

39. Potiphar put Joseph in charge of his house. His wife tried to seduce Joseph, then lied about it, so Potiphar put Joseph in prison.

40. Pharaoh put his cupbearer and baker in prison. Joseph interpreted their dreams. The cupbearer was restored but the baker was hanged.

41. Pharaoh had a dream and called for Joseph to interpret it. The dream predicted a famine. Pharaoh put Joseph in charge of all Egypt.

42. Joseph's brothers went to Egypt to buy grain but didn't recognise him. He kept Simeon in prison and sent the rest to fetch Benjamin.

43. When the grain ran out, Joseph's brothers went back to Egypt with Benjamin. Joseph invited them to his house and gave them a feast.

44. Joseph hid his cup in Benjamin's sack, then sent a steward after his brothers. Judah offered himself as a slave instead of Benjamin.

45. Joseph told his brothers who he was. They were afraid, but he told them, "God sent me here." His brothers went to fetch their father.

46. So Israel set out with all his household. God told him not to be afraid. Israel and all his family came to Egypt and Joseph met him.

47. Pharaoh allowed Joseph's family to settle in Goshen. The famine continued and the Egyptians sold all they had to Pharaoh for food.

48. Jacob became ill, so Joseph took his sons to see him. Jacob blessed Joseph's sons as his own, putting Ephraim ahead of Manasseh.

49. Jacob gathered his sons and blessed each of them. He charged them to bury him with Abraham in the cave in Canaan, and then he died.

50. Pharaoh allowed Joseph to go and bury Jacob. Before Joseph died, he said that God would lead his people back to the promised land.

Exodus

1. The Israelites prospered in Egypt, but a new king arose and forced them into hard labour. He commanded that their baby boys be killed.

2. Pharaoh's daughter found a Hebrew baby by the river. She named him Moses. When he grew up, Moses killed an Egyptian and fled to Midian.

3. Moses saw a burning bush. God told him to lead the Israelites out of Egypt. Moses asked God his name and God said, "I am who I am."

4. The LORD gave Moses signs so that the people would listen. Moses was afraid, so the LORD sent his brother Aaron to speak for him.

5. Moses and Aaron told Pharaoh to let the Israelites go into the desert to worship. Pharaoh refused and increased their workload instead.

6. The LORD told Moses that he would lead the Israelites out of Egypt to the promised land. Aaron and Moses were from the tribe of Levi.

7. Moses and Aaron went to Pharaoh. Aaron's staff became a snake, then the LORD turned the Nile to blood, but Pharaoh wouldn't listen.

8. The LORD sent a plague of frogs on Egypt. Pharaoh begged for relief but then hardened his heart. The LORD sent gnats and then flies.

9. The LORD sent a plague on the livestock of Egypt, then boils and then hail. Pharaoh begged for relief but then his heart was hardened.

10. The LORD sent a plague of locusts. Pharaoh begged for relief but then his heart was hardened. The LORD sent darkness for three days.

11. The LORD said that he would send one more plague, and then Pharaoh would let the Israelites go: all the firstborn Egyptians would die.

12. The LORD told the Israelites to take Passover. That night all the firstborn Egyptians were killed. Pharaoh told the Israelites to go.

13. The LORD told the Israelites to consecrate their firstborns to him. He guided them as a pillar of cloud by day and of fire by night.

14. Pharaoh's army caught the Israelites by the sea. The LORD parted the waters and the Israelites crossed. The Egyptian army was drowned.

15. The Israelites sang: "I will sing to the LORD, for he has triumphed; horse and rider he has thrown into the sea." They camped at Elim.

16. The Israelites grumbled to Moses that they had no food, so each day the LORD provided quails and manna. They rested on the sabbath.

17. The LORD told Moses to strike a rock to provide water. Amalek attacked Israel, but as Moses held up his arms Joshua's army prevailed.

18. Moses' father-in-law Jethro came and offered sacrifices to God. He suggested that Moses appoint leaders to help him judge the people.

19. The Israelites camped near the mountain in Sinai. The LORD spoke to Moses on the mountain and made his covenant with Israel.

20. I am the LORD your God. Honour the LORD above everything. Keep the Sabbath. Honour your parents. Don't do wrong to your neighbours.

21. If you buy a Hebrew slave he shall go free in the seventh year. Whoever kills shall be put to death. Whoever injures shall compensate.

22. Whoever steals shall make restitution. If a man sleeps with a virgin he shall marry her. You shall not oppress strangers or the poor.

23. You shall not pervert justice. Each year you shall hold feasts. My angel will lead you and I will drive your enemies from the land.

24. The people said, "All that the LORD has spoken we will do", and they offered sacrifices. The LORD told Moses to stay on the mountain.

25. Tell the Israelites to make a sanctuary for me. Make an ark with a mercy seat and two cherubim. Make a table. Then make a lampstand.

26. Make a tabernacle of fine linen. Make curtains of goats' hair to cover the tabernacle. Make boards of acacia wood and a linen veil.

27. Make an altar of acacia wood with bronze utensils. Make a court for the tabernacle of fine linen hangings and bronze pillars.

28. Set apart Aaron and his sons to minister as priests. Make a breastplate, an ephod, a robe, a tunic, a turban and a sash for them.

29. Sacrifice a young bull and two rams to consecrate Aaron and his sons. Make daily sacrifices on the altar and I will dwell with Israel.

30. Make an altar for burning incense. The Israelites shall each give half a shekel. Make a bronze laver. Make anointing oil and incense.

31. I have filled Bezalel with the Spirit of God, with skill to make everything I have commanded. The seventh day is a Sabbath of rest.

32. While Moses was away the people worshipped a golden calf. Moses pleaded with the LORD for them, but then had three thousand killed.

33. Moses set up a tent of meeting. He said to the LORD, "Don't send us from here without your presence." The LORD passed near to Moses.

34. Moses made new tablets for the law. The LORD spoke to him and made a covenant with Israel. When Moses returned his face was shining.

35. Moses told the Israelites to keep the Sabbath. He called for craftsmen to make the tabernacle. The people gave gifts for the work.

36. The people gave more than enough. The craftsmen made the curtains. Bezalel made the curtains, the boards, the veil and the pillars.

37. Bezalel made the ark with its cherubim, the table, the lampstand and the incense altar. He made the anointing oil and the incense.

38. Bezalel made the altar of burnt offering, the laver and the court. Ithamar kept an inventory of the gold, silver and bronze used.

39. They made the ephod, breastplate, tunics, turban and sash for Aaron. Moses saw that it had all been made as the LORD had commanded.

40. Moses set up the tabernacle and brought the ark into it, as the LORD had commanded. Then the glory of the LORD filled the tabernacle.

Leviticus

1. Whoever brings a burnt offering should slaughter a bull, a sheep, a goat or a bird. The priest shall burn it on the altar to the LORD.

2. A grain offering should be fine flour with oil and incense. The priest shall burn a portion. The rest belongs to Aaron and his sons.

3. A peace offering should be from the herd or the flock. Slaughter it at the tabernacle. The priest shall burn it on the altar as food.

4. If anyone sins unintentionally they should slaughter a bull, a goat or a lamb. The priest shall burn it to the LORD to make atonement.

5. When anyone sins with an oath or becomes unclean they should confess it and bring a sin offering. A guilt offering should be a ram.

6. When anyone cheats a neighbour they should make restitution and bring a guilt offering. The fire on the altar shall never go out.

7. The meat of a peace offering must be eaten within two days. Do not eat fat or blood. The wave offering belongs to Aaron and his sons.

8. Moses gathered the people at the tabernacle. He made offerings on the altar and consecrated Aaron and his sons with oil and blood.

9. Aaron brought a sin offering and a burnt offering to make atonement. The glory of the LORD appeared and a fire consumed the offerings.

10. Nadab and Abihu offered strange fire, so fire came from the LORD and killed them. Aaron and his other sons stayed at the tabernacle.

11. You may eat animals with cloven hooves that chew the cud, and fish with scales and fins. Anything that touches a carcass is unclean.

12. A male child shall be circumcised on the eighth day. A woman who gives birth shall bring offerings after her days of purification.

13. If anyone has leprosy the priest shall declare them unclean and they shall live outside the camp. A leprous garment shall be burned.

14. If anyone is healed of leprosy they shall shave their hair and bring offerings. If a house has mildew the priest shall inspect it.

15. When a man has a discharge he is unclean. When he ejaculates he is unclean until evening. When a woman has her period she is unclean.

16. Once a year Aaron shall make atonement for the people. He shall bring one goat as a sin offering and release another as a scapegoat.

17. Anyone who kills an animal and does not bring an offering is guilty. The life is in the blood and I have given it to make atonement.

18. Don't have sex with a relative, a woman on her period, your neighbour's wife, another man or an animal. These things defile the land.

19. Be holy. Keep my Sabbaths. Don't turn to idols. Love your neighbour as yourself. Don't mix livestock. Do no injustice. I am the LORD.

20. Anyone who worships Molech, curses their parents, commits adultery or has sex with a man shall be put to death. You shall be holy.

21. A priest must not make himself unclean and must only marry a virgin. No descendant of Aaron with a defect may offer the offerings.

22. A priest shall not eat the offerings if he is unclean. No outsider shall eat the offerings. Offerings must be animals without defect.

23. Proclaim as feasts: Passover, Unleavened Bread, Firstfruits, fifty days later, the day of trumpets, the Day of Atonement and Booths.

24. Aaron is to tend the lamps and set out the bread before the LORD. An Israelite blasphemed so they took him outside and stoned him.

25. Every seventh year the land shall rest. Every fiftieth year shall be a jubilee, when property shall be restored and slaves released.

26. If you keep my laws I will give peace in the land and make you fruitful. If not I will scatter you, but I will not break my covenant.

27. If anyone dedicates a person or land to the LORD, you shall make a valuation. A tithe of everything from the land belongs to the LORD.

Numbers

1. The LORD told Moses to count the Israelite armies. The number of men over twenty years old was 603,550. The Levites were not counted.

2. The Israelites shall camp around the tabernacle: Judah to the east, Reuben to the south, Ephraim to the west and Dan to the north.

3. The Levites are to assist Aaron. I have taken them in place of every firstborn. The number of Levites over one month old was 22,000.

4. The Kohathites are to carry the most holy things. The Gershonites are to carry the coverings. The Merarites are to carry the frame.

5. Anyone who sins shall make restitution and add a fifth. If a man suspects his wife of unfaithfulness he shall take her to the priest.

6. Anyone who makes a Nazirite vow shall not drink wine or cut their hair. Aaron's blessing shall be: "The LORD bless you and keep you."

7. The leader of each tribe brought a grain offering, a burnt offering, a sin offering and peace offerings. Moses spoke with the LORD.

8. Present the Levites as a wave offering to the LORD and make atonement for them. I have set them apart to serve at the tent of meeting.

9. In the first month of the second year the Israelites kept the Passover. Whenever the cloud lifted from the tabernacle they journeyed.

10. Make two silver trumpets to direct the congregation. In the second month the cloud lifted and they set out as the LORD had commanded.

11. The people grumbled that they had no meat. The LORD was angry but he sent quails. He put his Spirit on seventy elders to help Moses.

12. Miriam and Aaron spoke against Moses. The LORD was angry and Miriam became leprous. Moses prayed and after seven days she returned.

13. Moses sent men to spy out the land of Canaan. Caleb said, "Let us go up," but the others said that the inhabitants were too strong.

14. The people grumbled so the LORD said that they would spend forty years in the wilderness. They went up to the land but were defeated.

15. There is one law for you and for strangers. Make an offering if you sin unintentionally. Anyone who sins defiantly shall be cut off.

16. Korah, Dathan and Abiram rose against Moses and Aaron. Moses said, "The LORD will choose." The ground swallowed up those with Korah.

17. The LORD told Moses to bring a staff from each tribal leader to the Tent of Meeting to stop the grumbling. Aaron's staff blossomed.

18. The LORD told Aaron: "I have given you the Levites to work at the Tent of Meeting. Everything that is devoted to the LORD is yours."

19. Burn a heifer outside the camp for the water of cleansing. Anyone who is unclean and does not cleanse themselves shall be cut off.

20. The LORD told Moses to speak to a rock to produce water but he struck the rock. Edom refused Israel passage. Aaron died at Mount Hor.

21. The people grumbled so the LORD sent snakes. Moses made a bronze snake and whoever looked at it lived. Israel defeated the Amorites.

22. Balak sent for Balaam to curse Israel. Balaam's donkey warned him. The Angel of the LORD said, "Go, but speak only what I tell you."

23. The LORD gave Balaam a word: "How can I curse whom God has not cursed?" Then at another place: "The LORD their God is with Israel."

24. Balaam gave a word: "How lovely are your tents, O Jacob." Balak was angry. Balaam said: "A star and a sceptre shall rise in Israel."

25. The people were unfaithful with Moabite women and worshipped their gods. Phinehas killed one couple and the LORD commended his zeal.

26. The LORD told Moses and Eleazar to take a census. There were 601,730 fighting men and 23,000 Levites. Only Joshua and Caleb remained.

27. The daughters of Zelophehad were given an inheritance. The LORD told Moses that he was to die. Moses commissioned Joshua as leader.

28. Bring offerings each morning and evening, on the Sabbath and on the first of the month. Celebrate Passover and the Feast of Weeks.

29. In the seventh month on first day sound the trumpets; on the tenth day make atonement; on the fifteenth day celebrate for seven days.

30. When a man makes a vow he must not break his word. When a woman makes a vow it shall stand unless her father or husband forbids it.

31. The LORD told Moses to take vengeance on the Midianites. The Israelites killed the men, burned their cities and divided the spoils.

32. Reuben and Gad asked to settle in Gilead. Moses agreed if they helped to conquer the land, so Reuben, Gad and Manasseh built cities.

33. The Israelites journeyed from Egypt. In the fortieth year Aaron died. They camped by the Jordan and the LORD said, "Take the land."

34. Your borders in Canaan shall be Edom, the Great Sea, Mount Hor and the Jordan. Eleazar and Joshua shall divide the land among you.

35. You shall give cities to the Levites. Appoint cites of refuge for anyone who has killed accidently. A murderer shall be put to death.

36. The clan of Gilead asked about Zelophehad's daughters. Moses said, "Daughters who inherit land must marry within their own tribe."

Deuteronomy

1. The words of Moses: We journeyed from Horeb. You would not go up to take the land, so the LORD said, "This generation will not see it."

2. We went into the wilderness. Thirty-eight years passed, then the LORD told us to cross by Moab. He delivered Sihon the Amorite to us.

3. The LORD delivered Og of Bashan to us. I gave Gilead to Reuben, Gad and Manasseh. The LORD said that I would not cross into the land.

4. Now, Israel, hear the commandments and obey them. You heard the LORD speak from the fire. Take care not to make idols. The LORD is God.

5. The LORD made his covenant with us: Have no other gods; Keep the Sabbath; Honour your parents. You shall do all that he has commanded.

6. Hear, O Israel: The LORD our God is one. Love the LORD with all your heart, soul and strength. Teach your children these commandments.

7. Make no treaty with the nations of the land. You are a holy people; the LORD has chosen you. He will drive out the nations before you.

8. The LORD led you in the wilderness and tested you. He is bringing you into a good land. Do not forget the LORD or you shall perish.

9. It is not for your righteousness that you will occupy the land. You rebelled and made the calf so I broke the tablets of the covenant.

10. The LORD wrote on new tablets. What does the LORD ask? That you fear him, walk in his ways, love him, serve him and keep his commands.

11. You have seen all that the LORD has done. Keep these commands so that you may live long in the land. There is a blessing and a curse.

12. Destroy the high places where the nations worship their gods. You shall bring your offerings at the place that the LORD will choose.

13. If a prophet or anyone else entices you away from the LORD they must be put to death. If a town has turned away it must be destroyed.

14. You may eat animals with cloven hooves that chew the cud. Bring a tithe from your fields to eat before the LORD and for the Levites.

15. Every seven years you shall cancel debts. Hebrew slaves shall go free in the seventh year. Set apart every firstborn male animal.

16. Celebrate the Passover in the month of Abib. Celebrate the Feast of Weeks and the Feast of Booths. Appoint judges in all your towns.

17. Anyone who breaks the covenant shall be put to death. Go to the priests with hard decisions. Appoint the king that the LORD chooses.

18. The priests shall eat the offerings made by fire. You shall not practise divination. The LORD will raise up a prophet from among you.

19. Set aside three cities so that anyone who kills accidently may flee there. A matter must be established by two or three witnesses.

20. When you go to war, do not be afraid; the LORD is with you. As you go to attack a city, offer terms, except to the cities of the land.

21. If a dead body is found, the city elders must cleanse the guilt. Give your eldest son his portion. A rebellious son shall be stoned.

22. If you find your neighbour's ox you shall return it. If a man falsely claims that his new wife was not a virgin he shall be punished.

23. No Ammonite shall enter the assembly of the LORD. When you go out to war the camp must be holy. Be careful to do what you have vowed.

24. If a man divorces his wife he must not remarry her. Do not withhold wages. Leave the gleanings of your harvest for widows and orphans.

25. A judge may give up to forty lashes. If a man dies and has no son, his brother shall marry his widow. You shall have honest weights.

26. Bring the firstfruits of the land to the LORD. Bring a tithe in the third year and say to the LORD, "Look down and bless your people."

27. Write the law on large stones. The Levites will say, "Cursed is anyone who does not keep the law," and the people will reply, "Amen."

28. If you obey the LORD he will bless you above all nations; if not, you will be cursed and the LORD will send a nation to destroy you.

29. You have seen all that the LORD has done so keep this covenant. If you break it the land will be cursed and the LORD will uproot you.

30. When you return to the LORD he will have compassion; he will circumcise your heart. I have set before you life and death. Choose life.

31. Joshua will cross ahead of you. Read the law every seven years. The LORD said, "The people will turn away. Write a song as a witness."

32. Ascribe greatness to our God!
The LORD's portion is his people;
They turned away so he spurned them;
But he will provide atonement.

33. Moses blessed Israel before his death: Let Reuben live; bless Levi's work; Joseph's land is blessed. The eternal God is your refuge.

34. Moses climbed Mount Nebo. There the LORD showed him the promised land. Then Moses died. No prophet has arisen in Israel like Moses.

Joshua

1. The LORD said to Joshua, "Arise, cross into the land. Be strong and courageous." So Joshua told the officers to prepare provisions.

2. Joshua sent two spies to Jericho. A prostitute called Rahab hid them, so they promised to spare her family. They reported to Joshua.

3. The Israelites camped by the Jordan. When the priests carrying the ark reached the river it stopped, so Israel crossed on dry ground.

4. The LORD told Joshua to set up memorial stones from the Jordan. When the priests brought the ark up to the bank the waters returned.

5. The LORD told Joshua to circumcise the men. They called the place Gilgal. Joshua met the commander of the LORD's army and bowed down.

6. The LORD said that the army should march around Jericho. On the seventh day they shouted and the walls fell. They destroyed the city.

7. Achan took some banned items. When the army went against Ai they were defeated. The LORD identified Achan and the people stoned him.

8. The LORD told Joshua to take the army against Ai. They set up an ambush and destroyed the city. Joshua read out the book of the law.

9. The Gibeonites sent envoys. They pretended that they were from far away and made a treaty. The Israelites found out but spared them.

10. Five Amorite kings attacked the Gibeonites. The sun stood still while the Israelites took revenge. Joshua defeated the whole region.

11. The kings of the north joined forces to fight against Israel but the LORD gave Joshua victory. So Joshua took the whole land.

12. Israel defeated the kings east of the Jordan under Moses and the kings west of the Jordan under Joshua. Thirty-one kings in total.

13. Now Joshua was old. The LORD said, "Divide the remaining land among the tribes." Moses had given land to Reuben, Gad and Manasseh.

14. Judah came to Joshua. Caleb said, "Moses promised me the mountain because I obeyed the LORD fully." So Joshua gave Hebron to Caleb.

15. Judah's land bordered with Edom to the south. Caleb took Hebron, Othniel took Kiriath-sepher but Judah could not defeat Jerusalem.

16. Joseph's land was from the Jordan to the sea. Ephraim's territory was within Manasseh's. Ephraim did not drive out the Canaanites.

17. There was a lot for Machir the firstborn of Manasseh and a lot for the rest of Manasseh. Manasseh did not drive out the Canaanites.

18. Joshua sent surveyors from the remaining tribes and then divided the land. Benjamin's lot was from Kiriath-jearim to the Salt Sea.

19. Simeon's lot was within Judah's. There were lots for Zebulun, Issachar, Asher, Naphtali and Dan. The Israelites gave Joshua a city.

20. The LORD said to Joshua, "Appoint the cities of refuge." So they set apart Kedesh, Shechem, Hebron, Bezer, Ramoth and Golan.

21. The Israelites gave cities and pasture lands to the Levites. So the LORD gave Israel all the land he had promised to their fathers.

22. Reuben, Gad and Manasseh went back to their land and built an altar. They reassured Phinehas that they had not turned from the LORD.

23. Joshua summoned Israel and said, "You have seen all that the LORD has done. Hold fast to the LORD or you will perish from the land."

24. Joshua said to the people, "Choose this day whom you will serve," and they replied, "We will serve the LORD." Then Joshua died.

Judges

1. Judah defeated the Canaanites and took Jerusalem. Joseph put Bethel to the sword. But the Canaanites were not driven out completely.

2. After Joshua's generation died the Israelites served Baals. The LORD sold them to their enemies but raised up judges to deliver them.

3. After Othniel died the Israelites did evil. King Eglon defeated them. The LORD raised up Ehud who thrust a sword into Eglon's belly.

4. Jabin and Sisera oppressed Israel. Deborah sent Barak against them and the LORD routed them. Jael drove a peg through Sisera's head.

5. Deborah and Barak sang: "When leaders lead and people are willing, praise the LORD! Blessed is Jael; Let your enemies perish, O LORD!"

6. The LORD gave the Israelites to Midian. The angel of the LORD told Gideon to save Israel and gave him a sign. Gideon gathered an army.

7. The LORD told Gideon to send away all but 300 men. The 300 crept into the Midianite camp. They blew trumpets and the Midianites fled.

8. Gideon defeated Zebah and Zalmunna and punished Succoth and Penuel. He refused to rule Israel. When Gideon died Israel served Baals.

9. Abimelech killed his brothers and ruled over Israel. Gaal rose against him. Abimelech destroyed Shechem but was killed by a millstone.

10. Again the Israelites did evil. The LORD sold them to the Philistines and the Ammonites. They cried out and put aside foreign gods.

11. Jephthah vowed to sacrifice whatever came out to meet him if he defeated the Ammonites. His daughter met him so he sacrificed her.

12. The Ephraimites attacked Jephthah. Jephthah and the Gileadites defeated them and caught survivors by making them say 'Shibboleth'.

13. The LORD gave Israel to the Philistines. The angel of the LORD told Manoah's wife that she would conceive. She named her son Samson.

14. Samson took a Philistine wife. He killed a lion and bees made honey in the carcass. He posed a riddle but his wife explained it.

15. Samson's wife married another man so Samson burned the Philistine crops. The Israelites bound him. He killed a thousand Philistines.

16. Samson loved Delilah. She had his hair shaved so he lost his strength and was captured. He died pulling down the Philistine temple.

17. Micah set up a shrine. There was no king so everyone did what was right in their own eyes. Micah appointed a Levite as his priest.

18. Spies from Dan stayed with Micah. When the Danites went against Laish they took Micah's idol and his priest. They named the city Dan.

19. A Levite came to Gibeah. The men of the city raped his concubine until she died. He cut up her body and sent a piece to each tribe.

20. The Israelites gathered to attack Gibeah. The Benjaminites defended the city but they were defeated and only 600 of them survived.

21. The Israelites grieved that a tribe would be cut off. They destroyed Jabesh-gilead and captured wives for the remaining Benjaminites.

Ruth

1. Naomi, an Ephraimite, lived in Moab. Her husband and two sons died so she returned to Bethlehem with her daughter-in-law, Ruth.

2. Naomi had a rich relative named Boaz. Ruth went to glean in his fields. Boaz gave her food and told his men to leave grain for her.

3. Naomi told Ruth to go and sleep at Boaz's feet. When Boaz awoke, Ruth said, "You are my kinsman." Boaz said that he would marry her.

4. Boaz settled the inheritance with another kinsman and married Ruth. Ruth bore a son, Obed. Obed was father of Jesse, father of David.

1 Samuel

1. Hannah had no children. She cried out to the LORD, "Remember your servant." She bore a son, Samuel, and took him to Eli the priest.

2. Hannah prayed, "The LORD humbles and lifts up." Eli's sons did evil but Samuel served the LORD. A prophet condemned the house of Eli.

3. The LORD called Samuel. Eli told Samuel to answer, "Speak, LORD." The LORD told Samuel that he was about to judge the house of Eli.

4. The Israelites were defeated by the Philistines and Eli's sons were killed. When Eli heard that the ark had been captured, he died.

5. The Philistines put the ark in their temple. Their god fell on his face before it. The city became cursed so they sent the ark away.

6. The Philistines sent the ark away with guilt offerings. The people of Beth Shemesh found it and rejoiced but some were struck down.

7. The ark was taken to Kiriath-jearim. The Philistines attacked Israel. Samuel cried out to the LORD and the Israelites defeated them.

8. The elders of Israel asked Samuel to appoint a king. Samuel warned them what it would mean. The LORD told Samuel to give them a king.

9. Saul went looking for his father's donkeys. The LORD told Samuel to anoint him ruler of Israel. Samuel invited Saul to eat with him.

10. Samuel anointed Saul and gave him signs. The Spirit of God came upon Saul and he prophesied. Saul was chosen to rule the Israelites.

11. The Ammonites attacked Jabesh-gilead. Saul gathered the Israelites and defeated the Ammonites. The people made Saul king at Gilgal.

12. Samuel said, "The LORD brought your fathers out of Egypt. Now he has given you the king you asked for. Fear the LORD and serve him."

13. The Philistines encamped at Michmash. Saul made offerings to the LORD by himself. Samuel told Saul that his kingdom would not last.

14. Saul's son Jonathan went against the Philistines and routed them. Saul made an oath that no one should eat but Jonathan was spared.

15. The LORD told Saul to destroy Amalek but Saul spared King Agag. Samuel told Saul that the LORD had rejected him. Samuel killed Agag.

16. The LORD sent Samuel to anoint Jesse's son David as king. The Spirit came upon David. Saul sent for David to play the harp for him.

17. A Philistine champion named Goliath challenged the Israelites. David killed Goliath with a sling and a stone. The Philistines fled.

18. Jonathan loved David. Saul set David over the army but became jealous and tried to kill him. David married Saul's daughter Michal.

19. Jonathan warned David about Saul. David escaped and fled to Samuel. Saul went after David but the Spirit of God made him prophesy.

20. David and Jonathan agreed a sign. Saul was angry with Jonathan when David was not at the feast. Jonathan told David, "Go quickly!"

21. Ahimelech the priest gave David consecrated bread and Goliath's sword. David fled to King Achish of Gath and pretended he was mad.

22. About four hundred men joined David. Saul ordered that all the priests be killed because they helped David. Only Abiathar escaped.

23. David and his men saved Keilah from the Philistines. Saul came to Keilah so David escaped. Saul gave chase but he was called away.

24. Saul went after David. David cut off a piece of Saul's robe but spared his life. Saul wept and said, "You shall surely be king."

25. Samuel died. Nabal insulted David so his wife Abigail pleaded for restraint. The LORD struck Nabal dead and David married Abigail.

26. Saul came after David. David took Saul's spear and jug while he slept but spared his life. David called out and Saul blessed him.

27. David lived among the Philistines to escape Saul. King Achish gave him Ziklag. David secretly raided the land while he lived there.

28. The Philistines gathered for war. Saul asked a medium to call Samuel. Samuel said, "The LORD will hand you over to the Philistines."

29. David and his men marched with Achish. The Philistine commanders said, "He will turn against us," so Achish told David to go back.

30. The Amalekites had raided Ziklag. The LORD told David to pursue them. David and his men rescued the women and divided the spoils.

31. The Philistines fought Israel. Saul's sons were killed. Saul was badly wounded so he fell on his sword. The Israelites fled.

2 Samuel

1. A man came and told David that Saul and Jonathan were dead. David sang: "The beauty of Israel is slain. How the mighty have fallen!"

2. David was made king of Judah. Abner made Ish-bosheth king of Israel. Their men fought and Abner killed Joab's brother Asahel.

3. Abner argued with Ish-bosheth and offered to support David. David asked for his wife Michal. Joab killed Abner and David mourned.

4. Ish-bosheth lost heart. His captains Rechab and Baanah killed him and took his head to David. David commanded that they be killed.

5. David was anointed king over Israel. He took Jerusalem and the LORD was with him. The Philistines gathered but David defeated them.

6. David brought the ark from Judah. Uzzah touched it and was struck down. As the ark came into the city David danced before the LORD.

7. The LORD said to Nathan, "Tell David: 'I will establish your house. Your son will build my house.'" David prayed, "Who am I, O LORD?"

8. David defeated the Philistines, the Moabites, King Hadadezer, the Arameans and the Edomites. He reigned over Israel with justice.

9. David heard about Jonathan's son Mephibosheth, who was lame. He restored Saul's land to Mephibosheth and had him eat at his table.

10. The King of Ammon humiliated David's servants and hired the Arameans for war. Joab defeated them and David defeated King Hadadezer.

11. David lay with Uriah's wife Bathsheba and she fell pregnant. He told Joab to have Uriah killed in battle. David married Bathsheba.

12. Nathan asked David, "Why have you done evil?" David pleaded with God but his child with Bathsheba died. Then Bathsheba bore Solomon.

13. David's son Amnon sent for his sister Tamar and raped her. Tamar's brother Absalom had his servants kill Amnon and then he fled.

14. Joab sent a wise woman to ask David to bring Absalom back. David agreed, but he would not let Absalom see his face for two years.

15. Absalom went to Hebron and sent out spies to proclaim him king. David fled, but he told Zadok and Hushai to return to Jerusalem.

16. Shimei cursed David but David spared him. Absalom came to Jerusalem. Ahithophel advised Absalom to sleep with David's concubines.

17. Ahithophel wanted to pursue David, but Hushai advised gathering Israel. Absalom listened to Hushai. Hushai sent a warning to David.

18. The servants of David defeated Israel. Absalom got stuck in a tree and Joab killed him. Ahimaaz and the Cushite ran to tell David.

19. The king mourned for Absalom. The men of Judah came to escort him back across the Jordan. Shimei and Mephibosheth came to meet him.

20. Sheba led the men of Israel to desert David. Joab killed Amasa and besieged Sheba at Abel. The people of Abel cut off Sheba's head.

21. There was a famine; so David sought the LORD. He let the Gibeonites kill seven of Saul's descendants. Israel fought the Philistines.

22. David sang: "The LORD is my rock; I called and he thundered from heaven; He delivered me from my enemy; I will extol you, O LORD!"

23. David's last words were: "My house is secure with God." David's mighty men included the three who brought him water from Bethlehem.

24. David numbered the people of Israel and then regretted it. The LORD sent a plague. David bought Araunah's field and made offerings.

1 Kings

1. David was very old. His son Adonijah exalted himself as king. When David heard he told Zadok and Nathan to anoint Solomon as king.

2. David charged Solomon to keep the law and to punish Joab and Shimei. Then David died. Solomon had Adonijah, Joab and Shimei executed.

3. Solomon married Pharaoh's daughter. He asked the LORD for discernment. Two women came before him and he judged between them wisely.

4. Solomon had officials and twelve governors. He ruled from the River to the land of Egypt. Men of all nations came to hear his wisdom.

5. Solomon sent to King Hiram: "I will build a house for the LORD. Cut down cedars for me." The workers prepared the timber and stones.

6. Solomon built the temple. The LORD said, "If you walk in my ways I will dwell with Israel." Solomon overlaid the temple with gold.

7. Solomon built his own house. Hiram made pillars, the sea and utensils for the temple of bronze. Solomon made the furniture of gold.

8. The priests brought the ark into the temple. Solomon said, "O LORD, if anyone prays toward this place then hear from heaven and act."

9. The LORD said to Solomon, "If you walk in my ways I will establish your throne." Solomon did not make slaves of the sons of Israel.

10. The queen of Sheba came to test Solomon. She gave him gold, spices and precious stones. Solomon excelled all the kings of the earth.

11. Solomon had many wives and turned to other gods. Ahijah told Jeroboam that the LORD would give him ten of the tribes. Solomon died.

12. Rehoboam refused to reduce the labour demands on Israel. So all Israel except Judah made Jeroboam king. Jeroboam made golden calves.

13. A man of God cried out against Jeroboam's altar. He disobeyed the LORD by eating at an old prophet's house and was killed by a lion.

14. Ahijah told Jeroboam's wife: "The LORD says, 'I will sweep away the house of Jeroboam.'" Rehoboam ruled Judah and Judah did evil.

15. Abijam ruled Judah and was not devoted to the LORD. Asa ruled and did right. Nadab ruled Israel and did evil. Baasha killed Nadab.

16. Elah ruled Israel and did evil. Zimri killed Elah but Israel made Omri king. Omri did evil. Ahab ruled and began to worship Baal.

17. Elijah told Ahab, "There will be no rain." Elijah stayed with a widow in Zarephath. The widow's son died but the LORD revived him.

18. Elijah went to Ahab and challenged the prophets of Baal. Baal gave no answer but the LORD answered Elijah with fire. Then rain fell.

19. Elijah fled from Jezebel. At Horeb there was a wind, an earthquake and a fire; then the LORD spoke. Elijah put his mantle on Elisha.

20. Ben-hadad attacked Samaria. Israel defeated the Arameans twice. Ahab made a treaty with Ben-hadad so a prophet spoke against him.

21. Naboth would not sell his vineyard, so Jezebel had him killed. Elijah said to Ahab, "Dogs will lick up your blood and eat Jezebel."

22. Ahab and Jehoshaphat planned for war. Micaiah said, "I saw Israel scattered. Your prophets are lying." Ahab was killed in battle.

2 Kings

1. Ahaziah consulted Baal-zebub. Elijah said that he would die. Ahaziah sent men to Elijah but they were consumed by fire. Ahaziah died.

2. Elisha followed Elijah. A chariot of fire appeared and Elijah went up to heaven. Elisha took Elijah's mantle and divided the waters.

3. Israel, Judah and Edom went to fight Moab. Elisha said, "The LORD will send water and give you Moab." The Moabites were defeated.

4. Elisha told a Shunammite woman that she would have a son. The child died but Elisha revived him. Elisha cleansed the food at Gilgal.

5. Naaman of Aram was a leper. Elisha told him to wash in the Jordan and he was healed. Gehazi asked for a gift and became leprous.

6. The king of Aram sent an army to capture Elisha but the LORD blinded them. Ben-hadad besieged Samaria and there was a great famine.

7. Elisha prophesied an end to the famine. Four lepers went and found that the Arameans had fled. The people plundered the Aramean camp.

8. Elisha told Hazael that he would rule Aram. Hazael killed Ben-hadad. Jehoram ruled Judah and did evil. Ahaziah ruled and did evil.

9. Elisha sent a prophet to anoint Jehu. Jehu killed Joram and Ahaziah. Eunuchs threw Jezebel out of the window and dogs ate her body.

10. Jehu sent a letter and had Ahab's sons killed. He killed Ahaziah's brothers and all the worshippers of Baal. Hazael defeated Israel.

11. Athaliah destroyed the royal family but Jehosheba hid Joash. Jehoiada had the army proclaim Joash as king and put Athaliah to death.

12. Joash ruled in Jerusalem and did what was right. The priests collected money to repair the temple. Joash was killed by his servants.

13. Jehoahaz ruled Israel and they were oppressed by Hazael. Jehoash ruled and Elisha told him to strike the ground. Then Elisha died.

14. Amaziah ruled Judah and did right. He challenged Jehoash but Judah were defeated. Jeroboam ruled Israel and restored the borders.

15. Azariah and Jotham ruled Judah and did what was right. Zechariah, Shallum, Menahem, Pekahiah and Pekah ruled Israel and did evil.

16. Ahaz ruled Judah and did evil. Aram and Israel attacked Judah so Ahaz sent a tribute to the king of Assyria. Ahaz set up an altar.

17. Hoshea ruled Israel. The king of Assyria invaded and settled the land. This happened because the Israelites rejected the covenant.

18. Hezekiah ruled Judah and did right. The Assyrians surrounded Jerusalem. Rabshakeh said, "Don't listen to Hezekiah. Come out to me."

19. Hezekiah prayed, "O LORD, save us." Isaiah said, "The LORD says: I will defend the city." That night the Assyrians were struck dead.

20. Hezekiah was sick but the LORD extended his life. Envoys came from Babylon. Isaiah told Hezekiah, "Everything will be taken away."

21. Manasseh ruled in Jerusalem and did evil. The LORD said, "I will bring disaster on Jerusalem and Judah." Amon ruled and did evil.

22. Josiah ruled and did right. He had the law read out and tore his robes. Huldah said, "The LORD says: You will be buried in peace."

23. Josiah destroyed the altars and high places and held Passover. He was killed in battle. Jehoahaz and Jehoiakim ruled and did evil.

24. The LORD sent raiders against Judah. Jehoiachin ruled and Nebuchadnezzer took all Jerusalem captive. Zedekiah ruled and did evil.

25. Nebuchadnezzar besieged Jerusalem. Nebuzaradan burned the temple and took the people into exile. Evil-merodach released Jehoiachin.

1 Chronicles

1. Adam, Seth, Noah, Shem, Eber, Abraham; Abraham's sons were Isaac and Ishmael; Isaac's sons were Esau and Israel. Kings ruled in Edom.

2. Judah's line led to Obed, Jesse and David. Caleb was son of Hezron; Jerahmeel was firstborn of Hezron. Caleb's line were the Kenites.

3. David had six sons at Hebron, four by Bathshua and nine others. Solomon's line led to Jeconiah, and then to the sons of Elioenai.

4. Reaiah's sons were the Zorathites; God blessed Jabez; Shelah's sons worked for the king. Simeon's line went to Gedor to seek pasture.

5. Reuben lost his birthright; his sons lived in Gilead. The sons of Gad and the sons of Manasseh lived in Bashan until the captivity.

6. Levi's sons were Gershon, Kohath and Merari. The musicians were Heman and Asaph. Aaron's sons made offerings. They were given cities.

7. Issachar's sons were 87,000. Benjamin's sons were Bela, Beker and Jediael. Ephraim's line led to Joshua. Asher's sons were 26,000.

8. Benjamin was father of Bela, Ashbel, Aharah, Nohah and Rapha; Ner's line was Kish, Saul, Jonathan; the sons of Ulam were mighty men.

9.   Jerusalem was resettled by Judah, Benjamin, Ephraim and Manasseh; there were priests and Levite gatekeepers. Kish was father of Saul.

10.   The Philistines fought Israel and Saul fell on his sword. The Israelites fled. Saul died for his unfaithfulness against the LORD.

11.   The elders anointed David king. David's mighty men included the three who brought him water from Bethlehem. Abishai led the thirty.

12.   Benjaminites and Gadites went over to David at Ziklag. David made them officers. People kept coming until there was a great army.

13.   David said, "Let us bring the ark back." As they carried the ark Uzzah steadied it and was struck down. David took it to Obed-edom.

14.   David had more children. The Philistines attacked; David inquired of God and when he heard marching in the trees he defeated them.

15.   David told the Levites to carry the ark. Heman, Asaph and Ethan were the musicians. The ark was brought into the city of David.

16.   They made offerings and David appointed singers. "Give thanks to the LORD; He is greatly to be praised!" Asaph ministered each day.

17.   The LORD said to Nathan, "Tell David: I will establish your house; your son will build my house." David prayed, "Who am I, O LORD?"

18.   David defeated the Philistines, the Moabites, King Hadadezer, the Arameans and the Edomites. He reigned over Israel with justice.

19. The King of Ammon humiliated David's servants and hired the Arameans for war. Joab defeated them and David defeated King Hadadezer.

20. Joab besieged Rabbah and David took the plunder. War broke out with the Philistines and David and his men killed the giants.

21. Satan led David to count the Israelites. God sent a plague and a destroying angel. David bought Ornan's field and made offerings.

22. David told Solomon: "The LORD has said that you will build his temple. I have provided materials." He ordered the leaders to help.

23. David made Solomon king over Israel. He organised the Levites into the sons of Gershon, Kohath and Merari to serve in the temple.

24. The sons of Aaron were priests. David organised the sons of Eleazar and Ithamar by lot. The rest of the Levites also cast lots.

25. The sons of Asaph, Heman and Jeduthun prophesied with music. 288 were trained in singing to the LORD. They cast lots for duties.

26. The sons of Obed-edom, Meshelemiah and Hosah were gatekeepers. Ahijah, Zetham, Joel, Shubael and Shelomith oversaw the treasuries.

27. Divisions of 24,000 men were on duty month by month. There was a chief officer over each tribe. Joab was the commander of the army.

28. David assembled the leaders and said, "The LORD has chosen Solomon to build his house." He gave Solomon the plans for the temple.

29. The leaders gave offerings. David prayed, "Yours is the kingdom, O LORD. Of your own have we given you." David died at an old age.

2 Chronicles

1. Solomon made offerings. God said, "What shall I give you?" Solomon said, "Wisdom to rule this people." So Solomon ruled over Israel.

2. Solomon sent to King Hiram: "Send me cedars and a craftsman for the temple." Hiram replied, "The LORD has given David a wise son."

3. Solomon started work on the temple. He built the portico, the main hall, the Most Holy Place, two cherubim, the veil and two pillars.

4. Solomon made an altar, the Sea, ten lavers, ten lampstands, ten tables and the courts for the temple. Huram made the furnishings.

5. The priests brought the ark into the Most Holy Place. The singers praised the LORD and the glory of the LORD filled the temple.

6. Solomon said, "The LORD has kept his promise." He prayed, "O LORD, if anyone prays toward this place then hear from heaven and act."

7. Fire came from heaven and the Israelites worshipped. The LORD said to Solomon, "If you walk in my ways I will establish your throne."

8. Solomon built cities. He did not make slaves of the Israelites. He appointed the divisions of priests and Levites to their duties.

9. The queen of Sheba came to test Solomon and gave him gold and spices. Solomon excelled all the kings of the earth. Then he died.

10. Jeroboam and all Israel asked Rehoboam to reduce the labour demands. He refused. Rehoboam still ruled Judah but Israel rebelled.

11. The LORD told Rehoboam not to attack Jeroboam. All the Levites came to Judah because Jeroboam set up idols. Rehoboam had sons.

12. Rehoboam was unfaithful to the LORD so Shishak attacked Jerusalem. Rehoboam humbled himself and the anger of the LORD turned away.

13. Abijah became king of Judah. He drew up battle lines against Jeroboam and said, "The LORD is our God". The LORD routed Jeroboam.

14. Asa became king. He did right in the sight of the LORD. Zerah the Ethiopian brought an army against Judah but the LORD routed them.

15. Azariah said to Asa, "The LORD is with you when you are with Him. Do not give up." The people made a covenant to seek the LORD.

16. Baasha fortified Ramah so Asa made a treaty with Ben-hadad. Hanani said, "You relied on Aram not the LORD." Asa became ill and died.

17. Jehoshaphat became king and was devoted to the LORD. He sent his officials to teach the law. He grew greater and built fortresses.

18. Ahab and Jehoshaphat planned for war. Micaiah said, "I saw Israel scattered. Your prophets are lying." Ahab was killed in battle.

19. Jehoshaphat returned to Jerusalem. He appointed judges and said to them, "Judge carefully, for with the LORD there is no injustice."

20. An army came against Jehoshaphat so he sought the LORD. Jahaziel said, "The battle is not yours but God's." The LORD set ambushes.

21. Jehoram ruled and did evil. Elijah wrote saying, "The LORD will send a plague." The LORD struck Jehoram with a disease and he died.

22. The people made Ahaziah king. He did evil and was killed by Jehu. Athaliah destroyed the royal family but Jehoshabeath hid Joash.

23. Jehoiada gathered the Levites and anointed the king's son as king. Athaliah was killed. The people tore down the temple of Baal.

24. Joash ruled and did right while Jehoiada lived. The priests collected money to repair the temple. Joash was killed by his servants.

25. Amaziah ruled in Jerusalem. After he slaughtered the Edomites he bowed down to their gods. He challenged Jehoash and was defeated.

26. The people made Uzziah king. He did right and became powerful. But he went to burn incense on the altar and was struck with leprosy.

27. Jotham became king and did right in the sight of the LORD. He built fortresses in the hills and conquered the Ammonites.

28. Ahaz became king. He made idols, so the LORD gave him to Aram and Israel. He shut the LORD's temple and sacrificed to other gods.

29. Hezekiah became king and did right. He told the Levites to cleanse the temple. He assembled the officials and they made offerings.

30. Hezekiah sent couriers throughout Judah and Israel saying, "Return to the LORD." Many gathered in Jerusalem to celebrate Passover.

31. Hezekiah assigned the priests and Levites to their duties. The Israelites gave a tithe. Conaniah was in charge of the offerings.

32. Sennacherib besieged Judah. Hezekiah and Isaiah cried out to the LORD and the Assyrians were struck dead. Hezekiah had great riches.

33. Manasseh became king. He did much evil and was captured by the Assyrians. Then he sought the LORD. Amon became king and did evil.

34. Josiah became king. He repaired the temple and had the law read out. Huldah said, "The LORD says: You will be buried in peace."

35. Josiah celebrated the Passover. He appointed priests to their duties and provided offerings. Then he attacked Neco and was killed.

36. Jehoahaz, Jehoiakim, Jehoiachin and Zedekiah ruled. Then Nebuchadnezzar burned the temple and took Judah captive for seventy years.

Ezra

1. Cyrus said, "Let the LORD's people go up to Jerusalem and rebuild the temple." He gave the articles from the temple to Sheshbazzar.

2. The exiles returned to Judah with Zerubbabel. A total of 42,360 people returned. The heads of families gave offerings for the temple.

3. The Israelites made regular offerings. When the builders laid the foundation of the temple, the Levites sang praise to the LORD.

4. Enemies hindered the work in Judah. Rehum wrote to Artaxerxes: "Jerusalem is a rebellious city." So Artaxerxes stopped the building.

5. Zerubbabel began to build the temple. Tattenai wrote to Darius: "The elders say that Cyrus issued a decree to rebuild this temple."

6. Darius issued a decree: "The cost of the temple shall come from the treasury." The temple was completed and the Israelites celebrated.

7. Ezra went up to Jerusalem to teach the law. Artaxerxes wrote: "I decree that whatever Ezra needs shall be done." So I was encouraged.

8. I assembled the family heads from Babylon and gave the gifts for the temple to the Levites. We came to Jerusalem and made offerings.

9. The leaders told me that the people had taken foreign wives. I tore my robe and prayed, "O God, we have forsaken your commandments."

10. The Israelites wept. They all assembled and Ezra said, "Separate from your foreign wives." The family heads investigated the matter.

Nehemiah

1. The words of Nehemiah: Men from Judah said, "The wall of Jerusalem is broken down." I prayed, "O LORD, give me favour with the king."

2. The king granted my request to go and rebuild Jerusalem. Sanballat was displeased. I inspected the walls and said, "Let us rebuild."

3. The priests rebuilt the Sheep Gate, the Tekoites made repairs, Jedaiah repaired opposite his house, Meremoth repaired another section.

4. Sanballat ridiculed us and plotted to attack Jerusalem. So we prayed and posted a guard. The builders carried swords as they worked.

5. The people cried out, "We have to borrow to get grain." I told the nobles, "Let us stop exacting usury." I did not take my allowance.

6. Sanballat and Tobiah sent for me to do me harm. I replied, "Why should I come?" The wall was finished and our enemies were afraid.

7. I gave Hanani and Hananiah charge over Jerusalem. I registered the nobles, rulers and people by genealogy. The assembly was 42,360.

8. The people gathered and Ezra read from the law. Nehemiah said, "This day is holy. Do not mourn." The people held the Feast of Booths.

9. The Israelites confessed. The Levites said, "LORD, you brought our fathers out of Egypt. They rebelled but you did not forsake them."

10. The leaders sealed a covenant. The people made an oath: "We will not marry foreigners. We will bring the offerings for the temple."

11. The leaders and one in ten of the people lived in Jerusalem. There were descendants of Judah and of Benjamin, priests and Levites.

12. All the Levites and leaders gathered to dedicate the wall. They made offerings and rejoiced. Men were appointed over the storerooms.

13. I cleared Tobiah out of the temple. I confronted those who profaned the Sabbath and who married foreign women. Remember me, O God.

Esther

1. King Ahasuerus gave a feast for all his officials. Queen Vashti refused to come to him, so the wise men advised him to replace her.

2. Mordecai raised Esther. She was taken into the king's harem and was chosen as queen. Mordecai told Esther of a plot against the king.

3. Ahasuerus promoted Haman, but Mordecai would not bow to him. Haman asked to destroy the Jews. The king gave his seal for the decree.

4. Mordecai asked Esther to plead with the king. Esther said, "Hold a fast. I will go to the king against the law, and if I die, I die."

5. Esther won favour with the king. She said, "Let the king and Haman come to a feast tomorrow." Haman built a gallows to hang Mordecai.

6. That night the king read about the plot against him. Haman came to ask about hanging Mordecai. The king told Haman to honour Mordecai.

7. At the feast, the king asked Esther, "What is your request?" She said, "My people have been sold by Haman." The king had Haman hanged.

8. The king gave his ring to Mordecai. Mordecai sent letters to the provinces allowing the Jews to defend themselves. The Jews rejoiced.

9. On the day of the king's decree, the Jews destroyed their enemies. Mordecai wrote to all the Jews and established the Feast of Purim.

10. Mordecai the Jew was second only to King Ahasuerus.

Job

1. Job was blameless. The LORD allowed Satan to test him. Job's servants and children were killed. He tore his robes and worshipped.

2. Satan struck Job with boils. Job's wife told him to curse God. But Job did not sin. Eliphaz, Bildad and Zophar came to comfort him.

3. Job said, "Curse the day I was born! Why did I not die at birth? Why is light given to him who suffers? I have no rest, only turmoil."

4. Eliphaz said, "Will you become impatient? When did the innocent ever perish? I heard a voice: 'Can a man be more righteous than God?'"

5. "Who will answer you? Man is born to trouble. As for me, I would seek God. Do not despise his discipline. He wounds, but he binds up."

6. Job said, "My misery would outweigh the sand of the seas! You have proved no help. Show me how I have been wrong! Would I lie to you?"

7. "O God, my life is but a breath! Therefore I will speak out. What is man, that you examine him? Why have you set me as your target?"

8. Bildad said, "Does God pervert justice? Learn from past generations. He will not reject the blameless, nor will he uphold evildoers."

9. Job said, "How can a man dispute with God? His power is vast! But he destroys the innocent. If only there were a mediator between us!"

10. "God, why do you reject the work of your hands? You know that I am not guilty! Why did you bring me out of the womb? Leave me alone."

11. Zophar said, "Should your babble go unanswered? God exacts less than your guilt deserves! Reach out to him and you will find hope."

12. Job said, "Who does not know all these things? With God are wisdom and power. He brings darkness into light. He destroys nations."

13. "I want to argue my case with God. Be quiet and I will speak. Though he slay me, I will hope in him.

God, why do you hide your face?"

14. "Man is like a fleeting shadow. If a tree is cut down, it will sprout again, but will a man live again? You overpower him forever."

15. Eliphaz said, "Your own mouth condemns you! Why do you turn against God? The wicked will be like a vine stripped of unripe grapes."

16. Job said, "You're miserable comforters! God has torn me and shattered me. But my prayer is pure. Even now, my advocate is on high!"

17. "My spirit is broken. He has made me a byword. But come again all of you! I will not find a wise man among you. Where is my hope?"

18. Bildad said, "Why are we stupid in your sight? Indeed, the light of the wicked goes out. His roots dry up and his branches wither."

19. Job said, "How long will you torment me? God counts me as an enemy. My closest friends abhor me. But I know that my redeemer lives!"

20. Zophar said, "My understanding inspires me to answer. The triumph of the wicked is short. His food will turn sour in his stomach."

21. Job said, "Listen to me. Why do the wicked grow mighty? How often do they have trouble? Who repays them? Your answers are empty!"

22. Eliphaz said, "Is not your wickedness great? You withheld bread from the hungry. Is not God high? Submit to him and be at peace."

23. Job said, "If only I knew where to find God! When he has tested me, I shall come forth as gold. But he does whatever he pleases."

24. "The wounded cry out, but God charges no one with wrong. Some rebel against the light; they are exalted a while, and then are gone."

25. Bildad said, "Dominion and awe belong to God. Who can be righteous before him? Even the stars are not pure in his sight!"

26. Job said, "How you have helped the weak! Sheol is naked to God. The pillars of heaven tremble. These are the fringes of his ways!"

27. "My heart does not reproach me. Let my enemy be as the wicked! His many sons are for the sword. The wind sweeps him from his place."

28. "There is a mine for silver, but where is wisdom found? It is hidden from the eyes of all living. The fear of the Lord is wisdom!"

29. "Oh, for the days when God watched over me! When I took my seat in the square. I was father to the needy and comforted the mourners."

30. "But now younger men mock me. They do not hesitate to spit at me. God has cast me into the mire. When I expected good, evil came."

31. "Does God not see my ways? Have I lied? Have I refused to help the poor? Have I put my trust in money? Let the Almighty answer me!"

32. Elihu was angry with Job and his three friends. He said, "I am young, but it is not only the old who are wise. I will have my say."

33. "Job, please listen to my words. God does speak, perhaps in a dream or through pain. He does this to deliver a person from the pit."

34. "It is unthinkable that God would do wrong. Can one who hates justice govern? God shows no partiality. Job speaks like the wicked!"

35. "Even if you are righteous, what do you give to God? He does not answer because of the pride of evil men. You must wait for him!"

36. "I have more to say on God's behalf. He is mighty but does not despise any. Who is a teacher like him? Remember to extol his work!"

37. "God thunders with his voice. By the breath of God, ice is made. Do you know his wondrous works? He is great in power and justice!"

38. Then the LORD said, "I will question you. Where were you when I founded the earth? Who enclosed the sea? Can you bind the Pleiades?"

39. "Do you mark when the deer is born? Will the wild ox serve you? Do you give the horse his might? Does the hawk fly by your wisdom?"

40. Job said, "I have no answer."

The LORD said, "Will you condemn me? Behold now, Behemoth, which I made. Can anyone pierce his nose?"

41. "Can you catch Leviathan with a hook? Everything under heaven is mine. His breath sets coals ablaze. He is king over all the proud."

42. Job said, "I repent in ashes."

The LORD said to Eliphaz, "You have not spoken rightly of me, as Job has."

He restored Job's fortunes.

Psalms

1. Blessed is the man who does not walk with the wicked,
    whose delight is in the law of the LORD.
   He is like a tree planted by the water.

2. Why do the rulers plot against the LORD
    and his anointed?
   The LORD laughs!
   He said to me, "You are my son."
   O kings, fear the LORD!

3. O LORD, how many are my foes!
   But you are a shield around me.
   You have broken the teeth of the wicked.
   Salvation belongs to the LORD!

4. Answer me when I call, O God!
   O people, how long will you seek lies?
   Put your trust in the LORD!
   O LORD, you make me sleep in safety.

5. Hear my cry, O LORD!
   You hate all evildoers.
   Lead me in righteousness because of my enemies.
   Let all who take refuge in you rejoice!

6. Be merciful to me, O LORD!
   My soul is in anguish.
   I flood my bed with tears.
   Depart from me, you evildoers!
   The LORD has heard my cry.

7. O LORD, save me from all who pursue me.
   Arise in judgement!
   God has prepared his weapons against the wicked.
   I will praise the LORD!

8. O LORD, how majestic is your name in all the earth!
What is man that you care for him?
Yet you have crowned him with glory and honour.

9. I will praise you, O LORD!
You have rebuked the nations.
The LORD will judge the world with justice.
The needy will not be forgotten.

10. O LORD, why do you stand far off?
The wicked man hunts the weak.
He says, "God will never see."
O God, break the arm of the wicked!

11. In the LORD I take refuge.
How can you say, "Flee like a bird"?
The LORD hates the wicked.
The LORD is righteous and loves justice.

12. Help, O LORD, for the godly are no more.
Everyone lies.
"I will protect the weak," says the LORD.
The words of the LORD are pure.

13. How long, O LORD? Will you forget me forever?
Look on me and answer! Give light to my eyes.
But I will trust in your unfailing love.

14. The fool says in his heart, "There is no God."
There is no one who does good.
Will evildoers never learn? God is with the righteous.

15. LORD, who may dwell in your sanctuary?
He whose walk is blameless, who does not slander,
who keeps his oath even when it hurts.

16. Protect me, O God! I have no good besides you.
The LORD is my portion. I will not be shaken.
In your presence is fullness of joy!

17. Hear a just cause, O LORD.
    My steps have held to your paths.
    Hide me in the shadow of your wings.
    Deliver my life from the wicked.

18. The LORD is my rock.
    I called and he thundered from heaven.
    He rescued me from my enemy.
    I will praise you among the nations, O LORD!

19. The heavens declare the glory of God.
    The law of the LORD is perfect, making wise the simple.
    May my words be pleasing to you, O LORD.

20. May the LORD answer you in the day of trouble!
    May he remember your offerings.
    The LORD saves his anointed.
    We rise up and stand firm!

21. O LORD, the king rejoices in your strength!
    You set a crown upon his head.
    You will destroy your enemies.
    We will praise your power!

22. My God, why have you forsaken me?
    I am despised. They have pierced my hands.
    You have answered me!
    The nations will worship the LORD!

23. The LORD is my shepherd.
    He leads me in paths of righteousness.
    I will fear no evil.
    I will dwell in the house of the LORD forever.

24. The earth is the LORD's!
    He who has a pure heart will receive blessing.
    Lift up your heads, O gates!
    The King of glory shall come in.

25. To you, O LORD, I lift up my soul.
Show me your ways, teach me your paths.
Be gracious to me, forgive my sins.
I take refuge in you.

26. Vindicate me, O LORD, for I have walked with integrity.
I do not sit with deceitful men.
I love the place where your glory dwells.

27. The LORD is my light and my salvation.
My heart will not fear.
I will seek your face, O LORD; do not forsake me!
Wait for the LORD.

28. To you I cry, O LORD my rock.
Repay the wicked according to their works!
The LORD is my shield.
He is the strength of his people.

29. Ascribe to the LORD glory!
The voice of the LORD is over the waters.
The voice of the LORD shakes the wilderness.
The LORD is king!

30. I will exalt you, O LORD,
    for you spared me from going down to the pit.
I cried to you for mercy.
You turned my mourning into dancing.

31. In you, O LORD, I seek refuge.
Into your hand I commit my spirit.
Deliver me from my enemies.
Praise the LORD for his steadfast love!

32. Blessed are those whose sins are forgiven.
When I kept silent, my bones wasted away.
You surround me with glad cries of deliverance!

33. Rejoice in the LORD! Make melody, play skilfully.
Let all the earth fear the LORD.
His eye is on those who hope in his steadfast love.

34. O magnify the LORD with me!
I sought him and he answered.
Taste and see that the LORD is good.
He is close to the brokenhearted.

35. O LORD, fight against those who fight against me!
Then I will rejoice.
They repay evil for good.
Vindicate me in your righteousness!

36. The wicked flatter themselves.
Your love, O LORD, reaches to the heavens.
In your light we see light.
There the evildoers lie fallen.

37. Do not be envious of evildoers,
for they will fade like the grass.
The righteous will inherit the earth.
The LORD is their stronghold.

38. O LORD, your arrows have pierced me!
My guilt has overwhelmed me. My strength fails me.
I confess my sin.
Do not forsake me, my God!

39. When I was silent, my anguish increased.
O LORD, what is the measure of my days?
My hope is in you.
Deliver me from my transgressions.

40. I waited patiently for the LORD.
He drew me up from the pit.
I delight to do your will, O God.
My heart fails me, but you are my help.

41. Blessed are those who consider the weak.
My enemies say, "When will he die?"
They gather slander.
But you, O LORD, have upheld me.

42. As the deer pants for water,
  so my soul longs for you, O God.
Your waves break over me.
Why are you downcast, O my soul? Hope in God.

43. Vindicate me, O God.
Why have you rejected me?
Send forth your light and your truth.
Why are you downcast, O my soul? Hope in God.

44. O God, our fathers have told us
  how you drove out the nations.
But now you have sold your people.
Awake, O Lord! Rise up and help us.

45. My heart overflows with verses for the king.
Your God has anointed you with gladness.
All glorious is the princess in her chamber.

46. God is our refuge.
We will not fear, though the earth give way.
The nations rage, kingdoms fall.
"Be still and know that I am God."

47. Clap your hands, you nations.
How awesome is the LORD Most High!
Sing praises to our God, sing praises.
He is king of all the earth.

48. Great is the LORD, and greatly to be praised!
The joy of the whole earth is Mount Zion.
O God, we ponder your love in your temple.

49. Hear this, all peoples!
Man in his pomp will not endure.
He is like the beasts that perish.
But God will ransom my soul from Sheol.

50. The Mighty One, God the LORD speaks:
"I will not accept bulls and goats
for you hate discipline.
Offer a sacrifice of thanksgiving."

51. Have mercy on me, O God!
Cleanse me from my sin.
Do not cast me away from your presence.
A broken heart, O God, you will not despise.

52. Why do you boast of evil, O mighty man?
Surely God will bring you down to ruin.
But I am like a green olive tree in the house of God.

53. The fool says in his heart, "There is no God."
There is no one who does good.
Will evildoers never learn?
God has rejected them.

54. Save me, O God! For strangers have risen against me.
God is my helper. He will repay my enemies.
I will praise your name, O LORD!

55. Give ear to my prayer, O God.
My heart is in anguish.
It is my equal, my friend who rises against me!
Cast your burden on the LORD.

56. Be gracious to me, O God,
for my enemies trample on me.
Are my tears not in your book?
In God, whose word I praise, in God I trust.

57. Be merciful to me, O God.
I am in the midst of lions.
My heart is steadfast, for great is your love.
Be exalted above the heavens!

58. Do you rulers judge justly? No, you mete out violence.
O God, break their teeth!
The righteous will rejoice when they see vengeance.

59. Deliver me from my enemies, O God.
Each evening they return, howling like dogs.
Destroy them in wrath!
You, O God, are my fortress.

60. O God, you have rejected us, broken us. Now restore us!
God has promised: "Judah is my sceptre."
O grant us help against the enemy!

61. Hear my cry, O God!
Lead me to the rock that is higher than I.
Prolong the life of the king.
So I will ever sing praise to your name.

62. My soul waits for God alone.
He alone is my rock and my salvation.
Trust in him at all times, O people.
Power and love belong to God.

63. O God, you are my God.
   My soul thirsts for you.
Your love is better than life.
   My lips will sing your praise.
Liars will be silenced.

64. Hear me, O God!
Hide me from the plots of the wicked,
   who ambush the blameless.
God will bring them to ruin.
Let the upright be glad!

65. Praise awaits you, O God, in Zion.
By awesome deeds you answer us.
You silence the roaring seas.
You crown the year with abundance.

66. Shout for joy to God! Come and see what he has done.
He has not let our feet slip.
I will make an offering. God has heard my prayer.

67. May God be gracious to us,
and make his face to shine upon us.
Let the peoples praise you, O God!
The earth has yielded its increase.

68. Let God arise, let his enemies be scattered!
Kings and armies flee.
Our God is a God who saves.
Sing to him, O kingdoms of the earth!

69. Save me, O God! I endure scorn for your sake.
Rescue me from the mire.
My foes are all known to you.
Let your salvation protect me!

70. Make haste to help me, O God!
May those who seek my life be put to shame.
May all who seek you rejoice.
O LORD, do not delay.

71. In you, O LORD, I take refuge.
Do not forsake me when my strength fails.
I will tell of your righteousness.
I will praise you, O God.

72. Give the king your justice, O God.
May he defend the cause of the poor.
May all kings fall down before him.
Blessed be the LORD!

73. Surely God is good to the pure in heart.
I envied the wicked until I saw their end.
They are swept away.
God is my portion forever.

74. O God, why have you rejected us?
Foes have defiled your sanctuary.
How long will they mock?
You are king from of old. Rise up, O God!

75. We give thanks to you, O God.
"I say to the boastful, 'Do not boast.'"
God is the judge.
The wicked will drain the dregs of his cup.

76. God is known in Judah.
You are glorious, more majestic than the mountains.
The earth feared and was still
    when God arose to judgement.

77. In the day of trouble I sought the LORD.
Has he withdrawn his compassion?
You are the God of wonders.
Your path led through the sea.

78. God worked miracles in Egypt.
He brought his people to the holy land.
They rebelled and he rejected them.
He chose David to tend them.

79. O God, the nations have invaded
    and shed blood like water.
How long, O LORD? Save us for your name's sake.
Make your vengeance known!

80. Hear us, O Shepherd of Israel!
How long will you be angry? Restore us, O God.
Watch over the vine that you planted.
    Restore us, O God.

81. Sing aloud to God our strength.
I hear a voice: "I am the LORD.
Oh, that my people would listen to me!
I would subdue their enemies."

82. God judges among the gods:
"How long will you judge unjustly? Defend the weak.
You are all gods, but you shall die."
Arise, O God!

83. O God, do not keep silent!
Your enemies make plans against your people.
Edom, Moab, Amalek and Philistia.
Let them be put to shame.

84. How lovely is your dwelling place, O LORD!
A day in your courts is better
than a thousand elsewhere.
For the LORD is a sun and shield.

85. O LORD, you forgave the iniquity of your people.
Restore us again!
Surely his salvation is at hand.
Love and faithfulness will meet.

86. Hear, O LORD, and answer me. Save your servant!
You alone are God. I will glorify your name forever.
Show me a sign of your favour.

87. Glorious things are spoken of you, O city of God.
The LORD will write in the register of the peoples:
"This one was born in Zion."

88. O LORD, day and night I cry out to you.
You have put me in the darkest depths.
Do the dead rise up to praise you? I am in despair.

89. I will sing of the mercies of the LORD.
You said, "I will establish the throne of David forever."
O Lord, where is your love of old?

90. Lord, you have been our dwelling place.
All our days pass away under your wrath.
Return, O LORD!
Have compassion on your servants!

91. I will say of the LORD, "My refuge and my fortress."
His faithfulness will be your shield.
He will command his angels to guard you.

92. It is good to give thanks to the LORD.
How great are your works!
Your enemies shall perish.
The righteous flourish in your courts.

93. The LORD reigns!
Your throne is established from of old.
The LORD is mightier than the sea.
Holiness adorns your house forever.

94. O LORD, God of vengeance, shine forth!
How long will the wicked exult?
The LORD will not reject his people.
He will repay the corrupt.

95. Oh come, let us sing to the LORD!
He is the King above all gods.
Oh come, let us worship and bow down!
Do not harden your hearts.

96. Sing to the LORD!
Declare his glory among the nations. Worship the
LORD in holy splendour.
He will judge the world in righteousness.

97. The LORD reigns, let the earth rejoice!
Fire goes before him.
The heavens declare his righteousness.
Give thanks to his holy name!

98. Sing to the LORD!
He has remembered his steadfast love.
Make a joyful noise before the King.
He will judge the world in righteousness.

99. The LORD reigns, let the nations tremble!
The King loves justice.
He spoke from the pillar of cloud.
The LORD our God is holy!

100. Shout for joy to the LORD, all the earth!
Know that the LORD is God.
Enter his courts with praise.
For his love endures forever.

101. I will sing of justice, O LORD.
I will walk with integrity.
My eyes will be on the faithful of the land.
I will destroy the wicked.

102. Hear my prayer, O LORD; I wither away like grass.
You sit enthroned forever.
The heavens will perish, but your years have no end.

103. Bless the LORD, O my soul.
He forgives all your iniquity.
He has compassion on those who fear him.
Bless the LORD, all his works!

104. O LORD, you are very great.
You set the earth on its foundations.
All your creatures look to you for food.
Bless the LORD, O my soul!

105. Give thanks to the LORD!
He has remembered his covenant.
He sent Moses to perform signs.
He brought his people out of Egypt with joy.

106. The LORD is good!
We have sinned like our fathers.
They forgot their God. They served idols.
But the LORD remembered his covenant.

107. Oh give thanks to the LORD!
Let the redeemed say so.
He brought them out of darkness.
He stilled the storm.
He raises up the needy.

108. My heart is steadfast, O God.
Your love is great above the heavens.
God has spoken: "Judah is my sceptre."
Help us against the enemy!

109. Do not be silent, O God.
For wicked mouths speak against me.
May his name be blotted out!
Let curses come upon him!
Help me, O LORD.

110. The LORD says to my Lord:
"Sit at my right hand.
You are a priest in the order of Melchizedek."
The Lord will judge the nations.

111. Praise the Lord!
Great are his works.
He is ever mindful of his covenant.
All his precepts are sure.
His praise endures forever.

112. Blessed are those who fear the LORD.
Their righteousness endures forever.
They are not afraid of evil tidings.
The wicked melt away.

113. Praise the LORD!
Blessed be the name of the LORD forever.
He is exalted over all the nations.
He lifts the needy from the ash heap.

114. When Israel came out of Egypt,
Judah became God's sanctuary.
The sea looked and fled.
Tremble, O earth, at the presence of the Lord.

115. Not to us, O LORD, but to your name give glory.
Idols have eyes, but they cannot see.
O Israel, trust in the LORD. He will bless us.

116. I love the LORD, for he heard my cry.
When I was brought low, he saved me.
What can I give for all his goodness?
I will keep my vows.

117. Praise the LORD!
For great is his love towards us.

118. Give thanks to the LORD; for his love endures forever!
The nations surrounded me; I cut them off!
The LORD has become my salvation.

119. Blessed are those who walk in the law of the LORD.
Teach me your decrees. I love your commands.
Deliver me according to your promise.

120. In my distress I cry to the LORD.
Deliver me from a deceitful tongue.
Woe to me!
Too long have I lived among those who hate peace.

121. I lift up my eyes to the hills;
my help comes from the LORD.
He who keeps you will not slumber.
The LORD will keep you from all evil.

122. I was glad when they said,
"Let us go to the house of the LORD!"
The tribes go up to give thanks.
Pray for the peace of Jerusalem.

123. As the eyes of servants look to their master,
so our eyes look to the LORD.
Have mercy on us!
For we have endured much contempt.

124. If the LORD had not been on our side,
attackers would have swallowed us alive.
We have escaped.
Our help is in the name of the LORD.

125. Those who trust in the LORD are like Mount Zion,
which cannot be moved.
Do good, O LORD, to those who are good.
Peace be upon Israel.

126. When the LORD brought back the captives,
we were like dreamers.
He has done great things.
Those who sow in tears shall reap in joy.

127. Unless the LORD builds the house,
the builders labour in vain.
Children are a heritage from the LORD,
the fruit of the womb a reward.

128. Blessed are all who fear the LORD.
You will eat the fruit of your labour.
May the LORD bless you from Zion
  all the days of your life.

129. They have greatly oppressed me from my youth.
But the LORD has cut the cords of the wicked.
May all who hate Zion be put to shame!

130. I cry to you, O LORD!
If you kept a record of sins, who could stand?
But with you there is forgiveness.
O Israel, hope in the LORD!

131. My heart is not proud, O LORD.
I have quietened my soul,
  like a weaned child with its mother.
O Israel, put your hope in the LORD.

132. Remember, O LORD, how David vowed,
  "I will find a place for the LORD."
The LORD has chosen Zion:
  "This is my resting place forever."

133. How good it is when brothers live together in unity!
It is like precious oil upon the head.
There the LORD commanded his blessing.

134. Come, bless the LORD, all you servants of the LORD!
Lift up your hands to the sanctuary.
May the LORD bless you from Zion.

135. Praise the LORD! He is above all gods.
He struck down many nations.
Their idols are but silver and gold.
O Israel, bless the LORD!

136. Give thanks to the LORD,
  his love endures;
Who spread out the earth,
  his love endures;
Who led Israel out of Egypt,
  his love endures.

137. By the rivers of Babylon,
  we wept when we remembered Zion.
How can we sing the LORD's song?
O Babylon, happy the one who repays you!

138. I give you thanks, O LORD!
All the kings of the earth will praise you.
Though I walk in the midst of trouble,
  you preserve my life.

139. O LORD, you have known me.
Where can I go from your Spirit?
You knit me together in my mother's womb.
Search me and know my heart.

140. Rescue me, O LORD, from evildoers;
  protect me from the violent.
You are my God, my salvation.
The LORD executes justice for the poor.

141. O LORD, may my prayer be as incense.
Do not turn my heart to evil.
Let the righteous rebuke me.
Keep me from the traps of the wicked.

142. I cry out to the LORD!
When my spirit is faint, you know my path.
Save me from my persecutors!
You will deal bountifully with me.

143. Hear my prayer, O LORD!
My enemy has crushed my life.
My soul thirsts for you. Teach me the way I should go.
Destroy my adversaries.

144. Blessed be the LORD, who trains my hands for war.
O LORD, reach down and rescue me!
May there be no cry of distress in our streets.

145. I will exalt you, my God and King.
All you have made will praise you.
The LORD is faithful.
He is near to all who call upon him.

146. Praise the LORD, O my soul!
Do not trust in mortal men.
The LORD executes justice for the oppressed.
He watches over the fatherless.

147. It is good to sing praises to our God!
He counts the stars. He lifts up the humble.
Praise the LORD!
He declares his word to Israel.

148. Praise the LORD from the heavens!
Praise him, sun and moon!
Praise the LORD from the earth!
Young and old together, praise the LORD!

149. Praise the LORD!
Let Israel rejoice in their maker. The LORD takes
delight in his people.
Let swords be in their hands for judgement.

150. Praise the LORD!
Praise him with trumpet and strings!
Praise him with loud cymbals!
Let everything that has breath praise the LORD!

Proverbs

1. The proverbs of Solomon.

   My son, if sinners entice you, do not consent. Wisdom calls aloud. The complacency of fools destroys them.

2. My son, apply your heart to understanding. For the LORD gives wisdom. It will save you from the way of evil, and from the adulteress.

3. My son, trust in the LORD with all your heart. Do not despise his discipline. Wisdom is a tree of life. Do not quarrel without cause.

4. Listen, my sons: Get wisdom. The path of the righteous is like the morning sun. Guard your heart, for it is the wellspring of life.

5. My son, listen to my words. In the end an adulteress is bitter as wormwood. Keep away from her. Rejoice in the wife of your youth.

6. A little slumber, and poverty will come like a bandit. A scoundrel sows discord. My son, a man who commits adultery destroys himself.

7. My son, wisdom will keep you from the adulteress. I saw her seducing a young man. He followed her like an ox going to the slaughter.

8. Wisdom cries aloud: "My mouth speaks truth. The LORD brought me forth at the beginning of his works. Whoever finds me finds life."

9. Wisdom has built her house. She says, "Come, leave your folly." The fear of the LORD is the beginning of wisdom. Folly knows nothing.

10. A wise son makes a glad father.
Love covers all offences.
With many words, sin is not lacking.
The righteous will never be uprooted.

11. The LORD hates dishonest scales.
The wicked earn false wages.
Whoever gives water will get water.
Whoever trusts in riches will fall.

12. No one finds security by wickedness.
Those who work the land have food.
Rash words pierce like a sword.
Righteousness leads to life.

13. The righteous hate lies.
Hope deferred makes the heart sick.
Whoever heeds reproof is honoured.
Whoever spares the rod hates his son.

14. The talk of fools is a rod for their backs.
Even in laughter the heart may ache.
Those who oppress the poor insult their Maker.

15. A gentle answer turns away wrath.
The eyes of the LORD are everywhere.
Plans fail for lack of counsel.
The LORD hears the righteous.

16. A man plans his way, but the LORD directs his steps.
Kings detest evil.
Pride goes before destruction.
Wisdom is a fountain of life.

17. A wise servant will rule over a shameful son.
Starting a quarrel is like breaching a dam.
Even a fool seems wise if he keeps silent.

18. A fool delights in his own opinions.
The name of LORD is a strong tower.
A gift opens the way.
The tongue can bring life or death.

19. Wealth makes friends.
A false witness will not go unpunished.
A good wife is from the LORD.
Whoever helps the poor lends to the LORD.

20. Wine is a mocker, beer a brawler.
Even a child is known by his deeds.
The LORD hates false weights.
It is a snare to make rash vows.

21. To do justice is better than sacrifice.
Better to live on the roof than with a quarrelsome wife.
No plans can avail against the LORD.

22. A good name is better than riches.
Train a child and he will not go astray.
Incline your ear and apply your heart to my teaching.

23. Do not wear yourself out to get rich.
Do not move a boundary marker.
Buy the truth, and do not sell it.
Do not linger long over wine.

24. Do not envy the wicked.
Wisdom is sweet to the soul.
Fear the LORD and the king, my son.
I saw thorns in the field of the sluggard.

25. Do not exalt yourself in the king's presence.
If your enemy is hungry, give him food to eat.
To seek one's own glory is not glory.

26. As a dog returns to its vomit, so a fool repeats his folly.
Without gossip a quarrel dies down.
Whoever digs a pit will fall into it.

27. Faithful are the wounds of a friend.
A loud blessing in the morning will be taken as a curse.
A person is tested by being praised.

28. Better to be poor and honest than crooked and rich.
Whoever confesses sins will find mercy.
Whoever trusts in the LORD will prosper.

29. By justice a king builds up the land.
Whether a fool rages or laughs, there is no peace.
Correct your son and he will give you rest.

30. Every word of God is pure.
Give me neither poverty nor riches.
Four things are never satisfied:
  Sheol, a barren womb, earth and fire.

31. Speak up for the speechless.

Who can find an excellent wife? She buys a field, she makes garments, she watches over her household.

Ecclesiastes

1. Everything is meaningless! There is nothing new under the sun. I applied my heart to know wisdom, but much wisdom brings much sorrow.

2. I built houses, gathered possessions and sought pleasure. It was meaningless! The wise die like the foolish. I despaired of my toil.

3. There is a time for everything: to live, to die, to mourn, to dance. It is the gift of God that man should find pleasure in his work.

4. I saw the tears of the oppressed. Two have a good reward for their toil. I saw everyone follow a new king. This too is meaningless!

5. Do not make rash vows before God. The lover of money never has enough. What is gained by toil? It is good to find enjoyment in life.

6. Here is an evil: to have wealth and honour but not to enjoy them. What do the wise gain over fools? The more words, the less meaning.

7. The heart of the wise is in the house of mourning. Do not be too righteous, or too wicked. Men have gone in search of many schemes.

8. Obey the king's command. Though sinners do evil, it will be well for those who fear God. No one can know what goes on under the sun.

9. The same fate comes to all. A living dog is better than a dead lion. Enjoy the days of your vain life. Wisdom is better than strength.

10. A little folly spoils wisdom. Whoever digs a pit will fall into it. The lips of a fool consume him. Through laziness the roof leaks.

11. Whoever watches the clouds will never reap. You do not know what will prosper. Enjoy your youth, but know that God will judge you.

12. Remember your Creator in your youth, before the days of trouble come. Everything is meaningless! Fear God and keep his commandments.

Song of Songs

1. Let him kiss me! I am dark and lovely.
   Tell me, where do you pasture your flock?

   Follow the tracks, my love.
   Behold, you are beautiful.

2. She is a lily among thorns.

   He is an apple tree in the wood.
   Here he comes, leaping on the mountains.
   My beloved is mine and I am his.

3. By night I sought the one whom I love.
   I brought him into my mother's house.

   Behold, O daughters of Zion,
     the carriage of King Solomon!

4. You are beautiful, my love!
   Your eyes are doves, your breasts are like fawns.
   My bride is a garden.

   Let my beloved come to his garden.

5. My beloved is knocking!
   I opened to him but he had gone.
   The guards found me and wounded me.
   My beloved is ruddy, his body is ivory.

6. Where has your beloved gone?

   He has gone to his garden.

   You are beautiful, my love.
   Fair as the moon, awesome as an army with banners.

7. Your thighs are like jewels,
   your breasts like the fruit of a palm.

   May your kisses be like wine!
   Beloved, let us go into the fields.

8. Do not awaken love until it pleases.
   Love is as strong as death.

   Solomon had a vineyard, but mine is my own.
   Make haste, my beloved!

Isaiah

1. The LORD has spoken:
   I raised children but they have rebelled.
   Wash yourselves. I will smelt away your dross.
   Zion shall be redeemed.

2. The mountain of the LORD will be established.
   On that day the pride of men will be humbled.
   They will flee the splendour of the LORD.

3. The LORD will take away all support from Judah.
   Children will govern. You grind the faces of the poor.
   The women of Zion are proud.

4. In that day the branch of the LORD will be glorious.
   Those who are left in Zion will be called holy.
   The LORD will create a shelter.

5. Why did my vineyard yield wild grapes?
   Woe to those who pursue drink, who call evil good.
   The anger of the LORD is against his people.

6. I saw the LORD seated on high. A seraph brought a coal
   to my lips. The LORD said, "Who will go for us?" I said,
   "Here am I; send me!"

7. Aram plotted with Ephraim.
    The LORD sent Isaiah to King Ahaz:
    Behold, a virgin shall bear a son.
    The LORD will use Assyria as a razor.

8. The floodwaters of Assyria will overflow the land.
    Many will fall and be snared.
    I will trust in the LORD.
    They will curse their gods.

9. A child is born to us.
    His government will increase forever.
    The LORD will raise the enemies of Israel.
    His anger has not turned away.

10. Woe to those who rob the poor of justice.
    Woe to Assyria, whose purpose is to destroy.
    The remnant of Israel will return to the LORD.

11. A shoot will come up from Jesse.
    He will judge with righteousness.
    The wolf will live with the lamb.
    The Lord will gather his people.

12. In that day you will say:
     I will praise you, O LORD!
    Your anger has turned away.
    Surely God is my salvation. Sing for joy, O Zion!

13. The oracle concerning Babylon:
    Listen! The LORD is calling an army.
    I will punish the world for its evil.
    Babylon will be overthrown.

14. The LORD will again choose Israel.

    How you are fallen, O Lucifer!
    You will be cast away like a trampled corpse.
    Wail, O Philistia!

15. An oracle concerning Moab:
Ar of Moab is laid waste.
In the streets they wear sackcloth.
The waters of Dibon are full of blood.

16. A throne will be established from the house of David.
We have heard of the pride of Moab.
Within three years Moab will be despised.

17. An oracle concerning Damascus:
Damascus will become ruins. Jacob will be brought low.
You have forgotten the God of your salvation.

18. Woe to the land of buzzing wings,
  beyond the rivers of Cush.
The LORD will cut down the branches.
Wild animals will feed on them.

19. An oracle concerning Egypt:
I will hand the Egyptians over to a cruel master.
When they cry out to the LORD, he will send a saviour.

20. The LORD spoke through Isaiah:
As Isaiah has gone stripped for three years, so Assyria
will lead the Egyptians and Cushites captive.

21. The oracle concerning the wilderness of the sea:
I set a watchman. He said, "Fallen, fallen is Babylon!"
The glory of Kedar will end.

22. The oracle concerning the valley of vision:
The LORD has taken away the covering of Judah.
I will give to Eliakim the key of David.

23. The oracle concerning Tyre:
Wail, O ships, for Tyre is laid waste.
The LORD has planned it.
Tyre will be forgotten for seventy years.

24. Behold, the LORD lays the earth waste.
Its people are held guilty.
Fear and pit and snare await you.
The LORD of hosts will reign.

25. O LORD, I will praise you.
You have done marvellous things.
The LORD will swallow up death forever.
Moab will be trampled as straw.

26. A song will be sung in Judah:
The LORD is the eternal Rock.
Your hand is lifted high.
We gave birth to wind, but your dead will rise.

27. In that day the LORD will slay Leviathan.
By exile the guilt of Jacob will be purged.
Those who were perishing will worship the LORD.

28. Woe to the drunkards of Ephraim!
They will be snared.
Behold, I lay in Zion a precious cornerstone.
The LORD will do his alien work.

29. Woe to Ariel, the city of David!
But your enemies will be like dust.
I will astound these people.
No longer will Jacob be ashamed.

30. Woe to the stubborn children
   who seek help from Egypt!
The LORD will wait to show mercy.
The voice of the LORD will shatter Assyria.

31. Woe to those who trust in chariots!
As a lion roars, so the LORD will come down
   to fight for Mount Zion.
Turn back to him, O Israel.

32. Behold, a king will reign in righteousness.
Tremble, you women of ease.
The city will be deserted
  until the Spirit is poured upon us.

33. Woe to you, O destroyer!
The fear of the LORD is Zion's treasure.
"I will arise," says the LORD.
You will see the king in his beauty.

34. The LORD is enraged against the nations.
His sword is filled with blood.
He has a day of vengeance for Zion.
Edom shall lie waste.

35. The desert shall rejoice and bloom.
The eyes of the blind shall be opened.
The ransomed of the LORD
  shall return to Zion with songs.

36. The king of Assyria came against Judah. His
commander said, "Do not listen to Hezekiah. Have any
of the gods delivered their lands?"

37. Hezekiah prayed to the LORD.
Isaiah said, "The king of Assyria will not enter the city."
The angel of the LORD struck the Assyrians.

38. Hezekiah became sick, so he prayed.
The LORD said, "I will add fifteen years to your life."
Hezekiah wrote, "The LORD will save me."

39. The king of Babylon sent envoys. Hezekiah showed
them his treasure houses. Isaiah said, "All you have
shall be carried to Babylon."

40. Comfort, comfort my people.
   A voice cries: Prepare the way of the LORD!
   He is the everlasting God.
   He gives strength to the weary.

41. Let the nations meet for judgement.
   Do not fear, O Israel. I will help you. Idols are nothing.
   I will give a messenger of good news.

42. Behold, my Servant! He will bring justice to the nations.
   Sing to the LORD a new song.
   Hear, you deaf! The LORD gave Israel as spoil.

43. But I am with you, O Jacob.
   I am the LORD. There is no other saviour.
   Behold, I will do a new thing!
   Yet you have not called upon me.

44. I will pour my Spirit on your offspring.
   Who makes an idol?
   A carpenter prays to a block of wood.
   I am the LORD who made all things.

45. The LORD says to Cyrus:
   For the sake of Jacob I have called you. I am the LORD.
   Turn to me and be saved, all the ends of the earth!

46. The idols of Bel and Nebo are burdens to be carried.
   O Jacob, I have made you and I will carry you.
   I am God and there is no other.

47. Sit in the dust, O daughter of Babylon.
   You showed no mercy. You trusted in sorcery.
   Evil shall fall upon you. No one shall save you.

48. Hear this, O Jacob:
   I have refined you for my own sake.
   I am the First and the Last.
   Thus says your Redeemer: Go out from Babylon!

49. The LORD formed me in the womb
   to restore Jacob and to bring salvation.
Can a mother forget her nursing baby?
I will not forget Zion.

50. Have I no power to deliver?
The LORD has given me a learned tongue.
I gave my back to those who beat me.
He who justifies me is near.

51. Listen, the LORD will comfort Zion.
Awake, O arm of the LORD!
The ransomed shall return.
You will drink the cup of my wrath no more.

52. Awake, O Zion!
How beautiful are those who bring good news.
The LORD has redeemed Jerusalem.
Behold, my Servant will be lifted up.

53. He was despised and rejected.
He was pierced for our transgressions.
By his wounds we are healed.
Out of anguish he will see light.

54. Sing, O barren woman!
Your offspring will inherit the nations.
Your Maker is your husband.
No weapon formed against you will prosper.

55. Come, all you who are thirsty.
I will make an everlasting covenant.
My word will not return void.
The mountains will burst into song.

56. Keep justice, for salvation is near.
I will bring the outcasts of Israel to my house
   and gather still others.
The watchmen are blind.

57. The righteous find peace in death.
    As for you rebels, you make your bed wide.
    Let your idols save you!
    But I will not accuse forever.

58. You seek pleasure on your fast days.
    Is this not the fast I choose:
      to loose the bonds of injustice?
    Then your ruins will be rebuilt.

59. Your sins have separated you from God.
    Justice is far from us. Truth is nowhere.
    So the LORD put on garments of salvation and fury.

60. Arise, shine, for your light has come!
    The nations will come to you.
    I will make you majestic forever.
    Your God will be your glory.

61. The Spirit of the LORD is on me.
    He has sent me to proclaim freedom.
    My people will inherit a double portion.
    I delight in the LORD.

62. For Zion's sake I will not keep silent.
    You will be given a new name.
    Your God will rejoice over you.
    Raise a banner for the nations!

63. Why are your robes red?
    I have trampled the nations.
    Israel remembered who brought them through the sea.
    You, O LORD, are our father.

64. Oh that you would rend the heavens!
    You meet those who do right.
    We are all the work of your hand.
    Do not remember our sins forever.

65. I held out my hands to an obstinate people.
My servants will eat, but you will go hungry.
I will create new heavens and a new earth.

66. Listen! The LORD is repaying his enemies.
Rejoice with Jerusalem and be comforted.
All flesh will worship before me, says the LORD.

Jeremiah

1. The LORD said to me:
I appointed you as a prophet to the nations.
Do not be afraid. I am calling the northern kingdoms
against Judah.

2. Go and proclaim:
My people have exchanged their glory for idols.
You have all rebelled against me.
Now I will bring you to judgement.

3. Israel played the whore on every hill.
Her false sister Judah saw it.

Return, O faithless children!
Surely the LORD is our salvation.

4. Flee to safety!
I am bringing disaster from the north, says the LORD.

I have heard the trumpet!

The whole land shall be a desolation.

5. Israel and Judah have been utterly unfaithful to me.
I am bringing a distant nation against you.
Your sins have deprived you of good.

6.   Flee from Jerusalem!
I appointed watchmen but you would not listen.
An army is coming from the north.
My people are rejected silver.

7.   Proclaim at the temple:
Has this house become a den of thieves?
I sent prophets but you did not listen.
Judah will become desolate.

8.   Why do these people refuse to return?
They have no shame.

The LORD has doomed us because we have sinned.

Is there no balm in Gilead?

9.   No one speaks the truth.

I will scatter these people, says the LORD.
The sound of wailing is heard from Zion.
I act with justice.

10.   Do not learn the ways of the nations.
The LORD is the true God.

Listen, a great commotion from the north!
They have devoured Jacob.

11.   Both Israel and Judah have broken my covenant.
I will bring disaster.
Do not pray for them.
I will punish those who seek your life.

12.   O LORD, why do the wicked prosper?

I have left my house.
Many shepherds have ruined my vineyard.
I will uproot my evil neighbours.

13. The LORD told me to hide a sash in the rocks.
So I will ruin the pride of Judah, says the LORD.
All Judah will be carried into exile.

14. There is no water in the cisterns.
O LORD, do not forsake us!

I will destroy them by sword and by famine.
Can any idols bring rain?

15. Send these people away from my presence!
Who will mourn for Jerusalem?

O LORD, I suffer insult for you.

I am with you, says the LORD.

16. The LORD said to me:
Do not marry or have children.

Why has the LORD pronounced evil against us?

You have followed your evil hearts.

17. Cursed are those who trust in man.
Blessed are those who trust in the LORD.
If you keep the Sabbath, Jerusalem will remain forever.

18. The LORD said: Go to the potter.

You are clay in my hand, O Israel. My people have
forgotten me.

O LORD, they have dug a pit for me.

19. The LORD said: Buy a clay jar.
These people have burned sacrifices to foreign gods.
Then break the jar.
So I will smash this nation.

20. Pashhur put Jeremiah in the stocks.

Everyone mocks me.
But the word of the LORD is a fire in my bones.
Cursed be the day I was born!

21. Zedekiah enquired about Nebuchadnezzar.

The LORD says:
Whoever stays in the city will die.
Nebuchadnezzar will destroy it with fire.

22. Proclaim at the palace:
I will make you a desert.
Shallum will not return.
They will not lament for Jehoiakim.
Coniah is cast away.

23. I will raise up a righteous Branch, says the LORD.
The prophets fill you with false hopes.
I did not speak, yet they have prophesied.

24. The LORD showed me two baskets of figs after the exile
to Babylon. The good figs are the exiles. The bad figs are
those who remain.

25. You did not listen, says the LORD.
So I will summon Babylon.
Make the nations drink my cup of wrath.
The LORD will roar from on high.

26. The LORD said: Speak in the courts.

The priests seized Jeremiah to kill him, but the officials
refused. Uriah had been put to death.

27. The LORD said: Put a yoke on your neck.

I will hand all the nations over to serve
Nebuchadnezzar. Do not listen to your prophets.

28. Hananiah took Jeremiah's yoke and broke it.

The LORD said: Tell Hananiah, I have put an iron yoke on these nations.

Hananiah died.

29. Jeremiah wrote to the exiles:
Seek peace for the city.
After seventy years you will return.
Ahab, Zedekiah and Shemaiah speak lies.

30. Write these words in a book.
I will restore my people, says the LORD.
I have punished you but I will heal you.
I will be your God.

31. Sing with joy for Jacob! Return to your cities.
I will make a new covenant with Israel, says the LORD.
I will put my law within them.

32. Jeremiah bought a field in Anathoth.
O LORD, the city has been handed over to Babylon.
The LORD says: I will surely gather my people.

33. The LORD says:
I will tell you great things.
I will bring healing to the land.
David will never lack a son on the throne of Israel.

34. Tell Zedekiah:
You will not escape the king of Babylon.

The people took back their slaves.
The LORD says: You have not obeyed me.

35. The Rechabites refused to drink wine.

The LORD said to Judah:
The command of Jonadab has been obeyed, yet you have not obeyed me.

36. Baruch read out Jeremiah's words at the temple. The king sent for the scroll and burned it.

   The LORD said: I will bring disaster.

37. Zedekiah became king. Jeremiah said: Do not think the Babylonians will leave us. Irijah arrested Jeremiah. Zedekiah gave him bread.

38. Jeremiah was thrown into a cistern. Zedekiah sent for him. Jeremiah said: If you surrender to the king of Babylon then you will live.

39. The Babylonians besieged Jerusalem and captured Zedekiah. They took the people into exile. Nebuchadnezzar said: Do not harm Jeremiah.

40. Nebuzaradan said to Jeremiah: Go back to Gedaliah, who has been appointed over Judah. The captains warned Gedaliah about Ishmael.

41. Ishmael killed Gedaliah and eighty men. Johanan went to fight Ishmael but he escaped. Johanan led the survivors on the way to Egypt.

42. The people asked Jeremiah to pray.

   The LORD says: If you stay in the land, I will grant you mercy. If you go to Egypt, you will die.

43. Johanan and all the people did not obey the LORD. They went to Egypt.

   The LORD said: Nebuchadnezzar will ravage the land of Egypt.

44. The LORD says: Why do you provoke me with other gods? The people said: We will not listen. The LORD says: I am going to punish you.

45. When Baruch wrote these words, the LORD said to him:
I am going to break what I have built. Do not seek great
things for yourself.

46. Of Egypt:
There is no healing for you.
Prepare yourselves for exile.
I will deliver Egypt to Nebuchadnezzar.
But fear not, O Jacob!

47. Of the Philistines:
Waters are rising from the north.
The LORD is destroying the Philistines.
How can the sword of the LORD be quiet?

48. Of Moab:
Woe to Nebo, for it is laid waste.
We have heard of his arrogance.
How it is broken!
Moab has become a derision to all.

49. The LORD says:
Rabbah will become desolate. I will make Edom small.
Damascus has become feeble.
Flee, O Hazor. I will destroy Elam.

50. Of Babylon:
A nation will make her desolate.
Judah will seek the LORD.
Repay Babylon for all her deeds.
A sword against her warriors!

51. The LORD says:
I will send a destroyer against Babylon.
I will repay them for the evil done in Zion.

Read these words in Babylon.

52. Nebuchadnezzar besieged Jerusalem. Nebuzaradan burned the temple and took the people into exile. Evil-merodach released Jehoiachin.

Lamentations

1. How lonely sits the city!
   Judah has gone into exile.
   O LORD, I am despised.
   Is any sorrow like mine?
   There is no one to comfort me.

2. The LORD has not pitied Jacob.
   He has abandoned his sanctuary.
   My eyes fail with tears.
   Young and old lie slaughtered in the streets.

3. He has driven me into darkness.
   But the steadfast love of the LORD never ceases.
   Let us return to the LORD!
   You will repay my enemies.

4. The holy stones lie scattered.
   The children beg for food.
   The LORD has poured out his fierce anger.
   O Zion, your punishment will end.

5. Look, O LORD, and see our disgrace!
   We have become orphans.
   Slaves rule over us.
   But you, O LORD, reign forever.
   Restore us as of old!

Ezekiel

1. I saw visions of God. Out of a storm came four creatures. I saw wheels within wheels. Above them was a throne and the figure of a man.

2. He said to me: "Son of man, stand up." The Spirit entered me. He said: "I send you to rebel Israel." Before me was a scroll of woe.

3. He said to me: "Israel will not listen." I came to the exiles. The LORD said: "I have made you a watchman. I will open your mouth."

4. "Son of man, take clay and draw Jerusalem. Then lie on your side. You shall bear the punishment of Israel. Cook your bread over dung."

5. "Son of man, shave your head. Jerusalem has rebelled. A third shall die of famine, a third by the sword and a third I will scatter."

6. "Son of man, prophesy against the mountains of Jerusalem. The slain shall lie among their idols. They will know that I am the LORD."

7. "The end has come! I will punish you for all your abominations. Silver and gold cannot deliver. The people of the land will tremble."

8. The Spirit lifted me up. "Son of man, see what they do. Elders burn incense to idols. Women weep for Tammuz. Men worship the sun."

9. He cried, "Bring the executioners." Six men came. "Kill old and young, but do not touch those with the mark. I will not have pity."

10. He told the man in linen: "Take fire from between the wheels." Each wheel had four faces. The glory of the LORD left the temple.

11. The Spirit said: "These men plot evil." I said: "Will you destroy the remnant?" The LORD said: "I will put a new spirit within them."

12. "Son of man, they are a rebellious house. Bring out your baggage like an exile. I will disperse them. My word will not be delayed."

13. "Woe to the foolish prophets
who follow their own spirit.
I will send a storm in my wrath.
Woe to the women who sew magic charms."

14. The elders came to me. The LORD said: "They have set up idols in their hearts. Even Noah, Daniel and Job would only save themselves."

15. "Son of man, is wood taken from the vine to make anything? I have given it to the fire for fuel. So I have given up Jerusalem."

16. "Jerusalem, I made you flourish. But you played the whore. I will gather your lovers against you. Yet I will remember my covenant."

17. "An eagle planted a vine but it grew towards another eagle. Israel rebelled against Babylon with Egypt. I myself will plant a cedar."

18. "If a man is righteous, he shall live. If a son is violent, he shall die. I will judge each according to his ways. Repent and live!"

19. "Lament for the princes of Israel: A lioness had cubs. One was taken to Egypt, another to Babylon. A vine was stripped of its fruit."

20. "I led Israel out of Egypt. They did not walk in my law. I withheld my hand for my name's sake. You will know that I am the LORD."

21. "Son of man, prophesy against Israel.

A sword is sharpened!
Mark the way for the king of Babylon.
A ruin, ruin, ruin I will make it."

22. "A city that sheds blood.
In you they oppress orphans and widows.
Israel has become dross to me.
I will pour out my wrath upon them."

23. "Two sisters: Samaria and Jerusalem.
Oholah lusted after her lovers.
Oholibah was worse in whoring.
Bring an army and cut them down."

24. "Put meat into the pot. Woe to the bloody city!"

My wife died.

The LORD said: "I will profane my sanctuary.
Ezekiel will be a sign."

25. "To the Ammonites:
You jeered at Israel so I will destroy you.
I will judge Moab.
I will lay vengeance upon Edom and Philistia."

26. "Tyre jeered at Jerusalem so I will make her a bare rock.
Nebuchadnezzar will lay siege to you.
I will bring you to a dreadful end."

27. "Lament for Tyre:
Of oaks they made your oars.
Tarshish, Dedan, Judah and Damascus traded with you.
Now you are wrecked by the seas."

28. "To the king of Tyre:
You were perfect in Eden. You became proud.
I cast you to the ground.
There will be no more thorns for Israel."

29. "I am against you, Pharaoh, the great dragon.
Egypt will never again rule the nations.
Nebuchadnezzar will carry off its wealth."

30. "A sword will come upon Egypt.
Those who support her will fall.
Nebuchadnezzar will destroy the land.
I will break Pharaoh's arms."

31. "Assyria was a cedar.
It towered above the trees.
Its heart was proud.
Foreigners have cut it down.
This is Pharaoh and his hordes."

32. "Lament for Pharaoh:
You are a dragon in the seas.
The sword of Babylon will come upon you.
Elam and Edom are laid with the slain."

33. "Son of man, I have made you a watchman for Israel."

Jerusalem was struck down.

The LORD says: "I have made the land a desolation."

34. "Woe to the shepherds of Israel! They did not feed my
flock. I myself will seek my sheep. My servant David will
be their shepherd."

35. "Son of man, prophesy against Mount Seir:
Because you delivered Israel to the sword,
  blood will pursue you.
You will be desolate."

36. "Prophesy to the mountains of Israel:
I will make you inhabited again.
I will vindicate my name.
I will put my Spirit within you."

37. The LORD said: "Prophesy to the bones." The bones
became an army.

The LORD said: "Join two sticks. I will join Ephraim
and Judah."

38. "Son of man, prophesy against Gog:
You will come against my people.
My jealousy will be roused.
I will summon a sword against Gog."

39. "I am against you, O Gog.
I will give you a burial place in Israel.
Gather the birds for a feast.
Now I will have mercy on Jacob."

40. In visions the LORD brought me to a temple. He
brought me through the gates to the inner court. There
were tables for the offerings.

41. He measured the nave and the inner room. The side
chambers were in three storeys. In front of the Holy
Place was an altar of wood.

42. He led me to the outer court. The north and south
chambers are where the priests eat the offerings. He
measured all the temple area.

43. The glory of the LORD filled the temple. He said: "Son of man, describe the temple to Israel. The priests shall cleanse the altar."

44. "No foreigner shall enter my sanctuary. The sons of Zadok shall minister to me. They shall distinguish between the holy and unholy."

45. "Set apart a holy district for the LORD. The prince shall have land on each side. You shall have honest scales. Celebrate Passover."

46. "The prince shall bring offerings on the Sabbaths and New Moons. You shall offer a lamb daily." In the four corners were kitchens.

47. Water was flowing from the temple. He led me in until it was too deep to cross. The LORD says: "Divide the land among the tribes."

48. "Set a portion for each tribe. Adjoining Judah shall be the portion for the LORD. The name of the city shall be, The LORD Is There."

Daniel

1. Nebuchadnezzar brought the young nobles to Shinar. Daniel resolved not to defile himself with the king's food. God gave him wisdom.

2. Nebuchadnezzar had dreams. Daniel said, "God reveals mysteries. You saw a great statue broken by a stone. God will set up a kingdom."

3. Shadrach, Meshach and Abednego would not worship the gold statue. Nebuchadnezzar threw them into the furnace but God protected them.

4. "I, Nebuchadnezzar, dreamt of a tree cut down. Daniel said, 'You shall eat grass like an ox.' Afterwards my kingdom was restored."

5. Belshazzar drank from the temple vessels. A hand wrote on the wall. Daniel said, "Your kingdom is given to the Medes and Persians."

6. The satraps urged Darius to sign a law against prayer. Daniel prayed to God and was thrown to the lions. God closed the lions' mouths.

7. Daniel saw visions. I saw four great beasts. The Son of Man was given an everlasting kingdom. The fourth beast shall be destroyed.

8. I saw a ram with two horns. A goat with a large horn struck the ram. Gabriel said: "The ram is Media and Persia, the goat is Greece."

9. I read the book of Jeremiah. I prayed, "Israel has sinned. O God, forgive." Gabriel said, "Seventy weeks are decreed for atonement."

10. As I mourned I saw a man with a face like lightning. He said, "The prince of Persia delayed me. I came to explain the latter days."

11. "The king of the south will fight the king of the north. The king of the north will desecrate the temple. He will exalt himself."

12. "There will be a time of distress." I said, "How long?" He said, "Time, times and half a time. These words are sealed until the end."

Hosea

1. The LORD told Hosea, "Marry an adulterer for the land
    has prostituted itself."

    Gomer had sons.

    The LORD said, "You are not my people."

2. "Your mother has been unfaithful.
    I will expose her lewdness.
    Now I will speak tenderly to her.
    I will betroth you to me forever."

3. The LORD said to me, "Go, love your wife again as the
    LORD loves Israel." So I bought her back. For Israel will
    return to the LORD.

4. The LORD has a charge against Israel:
    "There is no faithfulness. They have left God to play the
    whore. The rulers love shameful ways."

5. "Hear this, O priests, O king! Israel shall stumble in his
    guilt. Ephraim is crushed in judgement. I will leave until
    they seek me."

6. Come, let us return to the LORD.
    On the third day he will raise us up.

    "I desire steadfast love, not offerings. Israel is defiled."

7. "The sins of Ephraim are revealed.
    They are like a heated oven. They call to Egypt, go to
    Assyria. Woe to them for they have strayed!"

8. "A vulture is over Israel. The calf of Samaria shall be
    broken. The LORD will punish their sins. For Israel has
    forgotten his Maker."

9. Rejoice not, O Israel!
    The days of punishment have come.
    "I will bereave them. I will drive them from my house."
    God will reject them.

10. Israel is a rich vine.
    The LORD will break down their altars.
    "Nations shall be gathered against them."
    It is time to seek the LORD.

11. "When Israel was a child, I loved him.
    But the sword shall devour them.
    How can I give you up, O Ephraim?
    I will bring them home."

12. "Jacob fought with God. Ephraim has said, 'I am rich.'
    But I am the LORD. I spoke through the prophets."
    The LORD will repay Ephraim.

13. "They make idols of silver. But I am the LORD.
    I will tear them open. Ephraim's sin is stored up.
    Shall I redeem them from death?"

14. O Israel, return to the LORD.
    "I will heal their apostasy. They shall blossom like the
    vine. Whoever is wise, let him understand."

Joel

1. What the locust swarm has left other locusts have eaten.
    The fields are destroyed.
    Lament, O priests! The day of the LORD is near.

2. A great army is on the mountains.
    Return to the LORD for he is merciful.
    "Fear not, I will restore you. I will pour out my Spirit."

3. "I will gather all the nations for judgement.
   For the day of the LORD is near.
   Jerusalem will be inhabited for all generations."

Amos

1. The LORD says: "I will punish Damascus. The remnant
   of the Philistines shall perish. I will send fire upon Tyre,
   Edom and Ammon."

2. "I will send fire upon Moab and Judah.
   I will punish Israel.
   They sell the poor for a pair of sandals.
   The mighty shall flee naked."

3. Does a lion roar when it has no prey?
   The LORD reveals his plans to the prophets.
   "On the day I punish Israel, I will punish Bethel."

4. "You cows of Bashan will be led away with hooks.
   I withheld the rain. I overthrew some of you.
   Prepare to meet your God, O Israel!"

5. "Fallen is virgin Israel. Seek me and live.
   You shall not dwell in your houses. I despise your feasts.
   Let justice roll like waters."

6. Woe to those who are at ease in Zion,
     who are not grieved over Joseph.

   The LORD declares:
   "I will raise up a nation against you."

7. The LORD showed me locusts, fire and a plumb line.

   Amaziah told Amos, "Flee to Judah." Amos said, "You
   shall die in an unclean land."

8. The LORD said:
"The end has come upon Israel.
I will not forget your deeds.
I will send a famine of hearing the words of the LORD."

9. The LORD said:
"Strike the pillars until the earth shakes.
I will sieve the house of Israel.
In that day I will restore my people."

Obadiah

1. The LORD says of Edom: "What disaster awaits you!
You stood aloof when strangers entered Jerusalem.
Saviours shall rule Mount Esau."

Jonah

1. The LORD sent Jonah to Nineveh. Jonah fled by ship. A
storm arose and the men threw Jonah into the sea. A
great fish swallowed him.

2. Jonah prayed: "I cried out in my distress. Waters
surrounded me. You brought me up from the pit!"
The fish vomited him onto dry land.

3. So Jonah went to Nineveh and said, "Nineveh shall be
overthrown!" The people fasted and wore sackcloth.
God relented of the disaster.

4. Jonah was angry and said, "O LORD, take my life." A
plant sheltered Jonah but it died. The LORD said,
"Should I not pity Nineveh?"

Micah

1.   The LORD is coming!
The mountains will melt.
"I will make Samaria a ruin."
Her wound is incurable.
Disaster has come to Jerusalem.

2.   Woe to those who plot evil!
The LORD says: "I am planning disaster.
My people have risen up like an enemy.
I will gather a remnant."

3.   You rulers tear the skin from my people.
The LORD says, "The sun will set for the prophets."
Zion will be ploughed up like a field.

4.   In the last days, nations will come to the mountain of
the LORD. Zion will be rescued from Babylon.
"I will give you horns of iron."

5.   "From you, O Bethlehem, will come a ruler."
The remnant of Jacob will be like a lion.
"I will punish the nations that did not obey."

6.   "O my people, have I wearied you?"
What does the LORD require?
Act justly and love mercy.
"I will make you desolate for your sins."

7.   The godly have perished from the earth.
But I will look to the LORD.
The nations will tremble.
Who is a God like you, forgiving sin?

Nahum

1. Against Nineveh:
   The LORD takes vengeance on his enemies.
   The LORD says, "I will break his yoke from you."
   Hold your feasts, O Judah!

2. The LORD is restoring Jacob.
   Chariots race through the streets.
   Nineveh is like a draining pool.
   "I am against you," declares the LORD.

3. Woe to the bloody city!
   "The nations will look at your shame."
   Draw water for the siege.
   Your shepherds are asleep, O king of Assyria.

Habakkuk

1. O LORD, why do you tolerate evil?
   "Behold, I am raising up the Chaldeans."
   Your eyes are pure.
   Why do you look upon the treacherous?

2. The LORD answered:
   "The just shall live by faith.
   Woe to him who plunders nations!
   What profit is an idol?
   The LORD is in his temple."

3. O LORD, renew your works!
   He stood and shook the earth.
   You crushed the head of the wicked.
   I will rejoice in the God of my salvation.

Zephaniah

1. "I will sweep away everything from the earth,"
   declares the LORD.

The day of the LORD is near.

"I will bring distress on mankind."

2. Seek the LORD, you humble.
Gaza shall be deserted.
The LORD is against you, O Canaan.
He will stretch out his hand to destroy Assyria.

3. Woe to the rebellious city!

"I have cut off nations.
I will leave a humble people."

Sing, O Zion!
The LORD will quiet you by his love.

Haggai

1. The LORD says:
"Consider your ways!
You never have enough
   because the temple lies in ruins."

So the people worked on the temple.

2. The LORD says:
"The latter glory of this temple
   shall be greater than the former.
This nation is unclean.
But now I will bless you."

Zechariah

1. The LORD said, "Return to me." So the people repented.

   I saw a man on a red horse. The LORD said, "I will return to Zion with mercy."

2. I saw a man going to measure Jerusalem. The LORD says, "I will be her glory."

   He sent me to the nations. The LORD will inherit Judah.

3. Joshua stood before the angel. The LORD rebuked Satan. They put new clothes on Joshua.

   The LORD says, "I will bring forth my servant."

4. I saw a lampstand. I asked the angel about it. "Not by might but by my Spirit," says the LORD. "Zerubbabel will complete the temple."

5. I saw a flying scroll. He said, "This is the curse on thieves and liars."

   I saw a woman in a basket. He said, "This is Wickedness."

6. I saw four chariots with red, black, white and dappled horses. The LORD said, "Make a crown for Joshua. He shall build the temple."

7. The people asked, "Should we fast?"
   The LORD said, "Show mercy and do not oppress. But they would not listen. So I scattered them."

8. The LORD said: "I am jealous for Zion.
   I will save my people. Your fasts shall be feasts.
   Nations shall seek the LORD in Jerusalem."

9. The LORD is against Hadrach, Tyre and Philistia.

Rejoice, O Zion!
Behold your king, riding on a donkey.
The LORD will save his people.

10. Ask the LORD for rain.
From Judah will come the cornerstone.
"I will save Judah for I am the LORD their God.
I will bring them home."

11. The cedar has fallen!
The LORD said, "Shepherd the doomed flock."
I broke the two staffs.
The LORD said, "Woe to the idle shepherd!"

12. The LORD said:
"I will make Jerusalem an immovable rock.
They will look upon me whom they have pierced.
And they will mourn alone."

13. "There will be a fountain to cleanse from sin.
I will remove prophets from the land.
Strike my shepherd and the sheep will scatter."

14. A day is coming when the LORD will go into battle.
Jerusalem will dwell in security.
All the nations will worship the LORD of hosts.

Malachi

1. "I have loved you," says the LORD.
"Where is my honour?
You offer blind and lame sacrifices.
My name will be great among the nations."

2. "Now, O priests, I will curse you.
   You have corrupted the covenant of Levi."
   Judah has profaned the sanctuary.
   The LORD hates divorce.

3. "My messenger will prepare the way.
   I will come to judge. You have robbed me of tithes.
   The LORD will remember those who serve him."

4. "The day is coming like a furnace.
   The sun of righteousness will rise.
   The wicked will be ashes.
   I will send you Elijah the prophet."

Matthew

1. The record of Jesus Christ, son of David, son of Abraham. Mary bore a son by the Holy Spirit. An angel told Joseph to name him Jesus.

2. Wise men came from the east to worship the child. King Herod ordered that all the baby boys be killed. An angel warned Joseph to flee.

3. John the Baptist was preaching, "Repent, the kingdom is near!" Jesus was baptised by John. A voice from heaven said, "This is my Son."

4. Jesus was tempted by Satan in the wilderness. He called Peter, Andrew, James and John to follow him. He preached and healed the sick.

5. Jesus said, "Blessed are the pure in heart. I have come to fulfil the law. Whoever is angry will be judged. I say, love your enemies."

6. "Do your good deeds in secret. Pray, 'Father, your kingdom come.' You cannot serve God and money. Do not be anxious about your life."

7. "Do not judge others. Do to others what you would have them do to you. Whoever obeys is like a man who built his house on the rock."

8. Jesus cleansed a leper. He healed the servant of a centurion who had faith. He calmed a storm at sea and cast demons out of two men.

9. Jesus healed a paralytic. Many sinners came to eat with him. He raised a girl to life and healed two blind men. The crowds marvelled.

10. Jesus sent out the twelve to proclaim the kingdom. "You will be hated for my name, but do not fear. Whoever receives you receives me."

11. John sent word from prison. Jesus said, "John the Baptist is Elijah." Jesus denounced the cities and said, "Come, my burden is light."

12. The Pharisees opposed Jesus when he healed on the Sabbath. He said, "A tree is known by its fruit. The sign of Jonah will be given."

13. Jesus gave a parable about a sower. He told the disciples, "Seeing they do not see." He said, "The kingdom is like hidden treasure."

14. Herod had John the Baptist killed. Jesus fed 5,000 men with five loaves and two fish. Jesus came to the disciples walking on the sea.

15. Jesus challenged the Pharisees about tradition. He healed a Canaanite woman's daughter. He taught on the mountain and fed 4,000 men.

16. Peter said, "You are the Christ." Jesus told them that he must be killed and be raised. He said, "Take up your cross and follow me."

17. Jesus took Peter, James and John and was transfigured. A voice said, "This is my son." Jesus healed an epileptic. Peter paid the tax.

18. Jesus said, "Become like children to enter the kingdom. A shepherd searches for the lost sheep. Forgive seventy times seven times."

19. Jesus was asked about divorce. He said, "Do not separate what God has joined." He told a rich man, "Sell everything and follow me."

20. "The kingdom is like a master paying wages." Jesus told the disciples, "The Son of Man came to give his life as a ransom for many."

21. Jesus rode into Jerusalem on a donkey. He healed and taught in the temple. "A man sent his son to his tenants, but they killed him."

22. Jesus said, "The kingdom is like a wedding." The Pharisees questioned him about the law. He said, "Love God and love your neighbour."

23. Jesus said, "The Pharisees preach but do not practise. You strain out a gnat but swallow a camel. You kill and crucify the prophets."

24. Jesus said, "In the end there will be tribulation. Let those in Judea flee. The Son of Man will come in glory. No one knows the day."

25. "The kingdom is like virgins awaiting the bridegroom. A man entrusted talents to his servants. The Son of Man will judge the nations."

26. Jesus took Passover with his disciples. He prayed in agony in Gethsemane. Judas betrayed Jesus to the chief priests. Peter denied him.

27. Jesus was handed over to Pilate. The crowd said, "Crucify him!" He was mocked and crucified. Darkness fell and he gave up his spirit.

28. The women went to the tomb. An angel said, "He has risen!" Jesus met them. He came to the eleven and said, "Go and make disciples."

Mark

1. Jesus was baptised by John. He called Simon, Andrew, James and John to follow him. He preached and cast out demons. He healed a leper.

2. Many gathered at the house. Jesus forgave a paralytic his sins and healed him. He was questioned about fasting and keeping the Sabbath.

3. Jesus healed a man on the Sabbath. Great crowds followed him. He appointed twelve apostles. He said, "Whoever obeys God is my family."

4. Jesus taught a parable about a sower and many others. He explained everything to the disciples. In the boat he calmed a great storm.

5. Jesus delivered a man of many demons. They entered a herd of pigs. He healed a woman with a haemorrhage and raised Jairus' daughter.

6. He sent the twelve out to preach. Herod executed John the Baptist. Jesus fed 5,000 men. He came to the disciples walking on the sea.

7. The Pharisees questioned Jesus about tradition. He said, "Evil comes from within." He delivered a Gentile girl and healed a deaf man.

8. Jesus fed 4,000 people and healed a blind man. Peter said, "You are the Christ." Jesus told them that he must be killed and rise again.

9. Jesus took Peter, James and John and was transfigured. He healed an epileptic. The disciples argued about which of them was greatest.

10. Jesus was questioned about divorce. He told a rich man to sell everything. He said, "The first must be last." He healed Bartimaeus.

11. Jesus rode into Jerusalem on a donkey. He drove the money-changers from the temple. The elders asked, "Who gave you this authority?"

12. Jesus said, "A man's tenants killed his son." The Pharisees questioned him about the law. He said, "Love God and love your neighbour."

13. Jesus said, "In the end you will be hated by all. Let those in Judea flee. The Son of Man will come in glory. No one knows the day."

14. Jesus took Passover with his disciples. He prayed in agony in Gethsemane. Judas betrayed him to the chief priests. Peter denied him.

15. Jesus was handed over to Pilate. The crowd cried, "Crucify him!" He was mocked and crucified. Darkness fell and he breathed his last.

16. The women went to the tomb. A man in white said, "He has risen!" Jesus appeared to the disciples. He said, "Go and preach the gospel."

Luke

1. The angel Gabriel foretold the birth of John. He told Mary, "You will have a son named Jesus." Mary said, "My soul magnifies the Lord!"

2. Mary gave birth in Bethlehem. Angels sent shepherds to see the child. Jesus was presented at the temple. He grew in wisdom and stature.

3. John came from the wilderness preaching repentance. Jesus was baptised. He was son of David, son of Abraham, son of Adam, son of God.

4. Jesus was tempted by Satan in the wilderness. In the synagogue he read out, "The Spirit of the Lord is on me." He healed all the sick.

5. Simon, James and John left everything and followed Jesus. Jesus forgave and healed a paralytic. The Pharisees asked him about fasting.

6. Jesus healed a man on the Sabbath. He chose twelve apostles. He said, "Blessed are the poor. Love your enemies. Hear and do my words."

7. Jesus healed a centurion's servant and raised a widow's son. John sent messengers to Jesus. A woman washed Jesus' feet with her tears.

8. Jesus told a parable about a sower. He explained it to his disciples. He calmed a storm, delivered a man and healed Jairus' daughter.

9. Jesus sent out the twelve. He fed 5,000 men. Peter said, "You are the Christ." Jesus said, "Take up your cross." He was transfigured.

10. Jesus sent out the seventy-two. A lawyer asked, "Who is my neighbour?" Jesus said, "A man was robbed. He was helped by a Samaritan."

11. Jesus said, "Pray, 'Father, your kingdom come.' Seek and you will find. Only the sign of Jonah will be given. Woe to you Pharisees!"

12. Jesus said, "Even the hairs of your head are numbered. Sell your possessions. Be ready for the Son of Man. I came to bring division."

13. Jesus said, "Repent or you will perish." He healed a woman on the Sabbath. He said, "Seek the narrow door. I must go on to Jerusalem."

14. Jesus said, "Choose the lowest place. A man gave a banquet but his guests made excuses. To be my disciple you must carry your cross."

15. Jesus said, "Heaven rejoices when a sinner repents. A son squandered his father's wealth. He returned and his father called a feast."

16. "A shrewd manager reduced his master's bills before he was fired. Abraham would not send Lazarus to comfort a rich man in Hades."

17. Jesus said, "If your brother repents, forgive him." He healed ten lepers. He said, "In his day the Son of Man will light up the sky."

18. Jesus gave parables about prayer. He told a rich man to sell everything. He said, "The Son of Man will be killed but he will rise."

19. Jesus ate with Zacchaeus. He told a parable about servants in the kingdom. He rode into Jerusalem on a colt and wept over the city.

20. The elders questioned Jesus' authority. Jesus said, "A man's tenants killed his son." So they asked about taxes and the resurrection.

21. Jesus said, "The temple will be thrown down. Jerusalem will be trampled. The Son of Man will come in glory. Stay awake at all times."

22. Jesus took Passover with the disciples. He prayed at the Mount of Olives. Judas betrayed him to the chief priests. Peter denied him.

23. Jesus was taken to Pilate. The crowd said, "Crucify him!" He was crucified with two criminals. Darkness fell and he breathed his last.

24. The women found the tomb empty. Jesus met two on the road to Emmaus. He appeared to the disciples and opened the Scriptures to them.

John

1. The Word of God became flesh and dwelt with us. John the Baptist bore witness to him. Andrew told Simon Peter and they followed Jesus.

2. Jesus turned water into wine at a wedding. He drove money-changers from the temple. He said, "Destroy this temple and I will raise it."

3. Jesus told Nicodemus, "Be born again. Whoever believes in the Son will have eternal life." John the Baptist said, "He is above all."

4. Jesus spoke with a Samaritan woman about her husbands. She said, "Can this be the Christ?" Many believed. He healed an official's son.

5. Jesus healed a man at Bethesda. He said, "The Son only does what he sees the Father doing. My works and the Scriptures bear witness."

6. Jesus fed 5,000 men and walked across the sea. He said, "I am the bread of life. My flesh is true food." Many disciples turned back.

7. Jesus went to the feast. The people said, "Is this the Christ?" The chief priests tried to arrest him. He called out, "Come and drink."

8. Jesus did not condemn a woman caught in adultery. The Pharisees questioned him. He said, "If God were your Father you would love me."

9. Jesus healed a blind man on the Sabbath. The Pharisees called the man and threw him out. Jesus said, "I came that the blind may see."

10. Jesus said, "I am the good shepherd. I give my life for the sheep." They asked, "Are you the Christ?" He said, "My sheep follow me."

11. Lazarus died. Jesus went to the tomb and said, "Lazarus, come out." Lazarus came out. The chief priests plotted to put Jesus to death.

12. Jesus rode into Jerusalem. The crowd shouted, "Hosanna!" He said, "The Son of Man must be lifted up. I have come to save the world."

13. Jesus washed the disciples' feet. He said, "One of you will betray me." Judas left. Jesus said, "Love each other as I have loved you."

14. "I am the way, the truth, and the life. I am in the Father and the Father in me. He will give you the Holy Spirit. Do not be afraid."

15. "I am the vine, you are the branches. You are my friends if you do what I command. If they persecuted me, they will persecute you."

16. "The Spirit will convict the world of sin. He will guide you into all truth. Your sorrow will turn to joy. I am going to the Father."

17. Jesus said, "Father, I have revealed your name to those you gave me. Sanctify them in the truth. May all who believe in me be one."

18. Judas betrayed Jesus to the chief priests. Peter denied him. He was sent before Pilate. Jesus said, "My kingdom is not of this world."

19. The soldiers took Jesus and crucified him. He said, "It is finished." He gave up his spirit. A soldier pierced his side with a spear.

20. Mary went to the tomb and found it empty. Jesus met her. He came and stood among the disciples. Thomas said, "My Lord and my God!"

21. Jesus appeared as the disciples were fishing. He said to Peter, "Do you love me? Feed my sheep." The beloved disciple has testified.

Acts

1. Jesus said, "You will receive the Spirit and be my witnesses." He was taken up in a cloud. The believers cast lots to replace Judas.

2. At Pentecost they were filled with the Spirit. Peter told the crowd, "You crucified Jesus but God has made him Lord." 3,000 believed.

3. Peter and John healed a lame man at the temple. Peter told the people, "Faith in Jesus has healed this man. Repent of your sins."

4. They were taken before the rulers. Peter and John said, "We cannot stop speaking about Jesus." The believers prayed for boldness.

5. Ananias and Sapphira told a lie and fell dead. An angel released the apostles from prison. Gamaliel advised, "Leave these men alone."

6. The disciples chose seven men to distribute food. Some from the synagogue disputed with Stephen. They took him before the council.

7. Stephen said, "Brothers, God called Abraham and appeared to Moses. You killed the Righteous One." They were enraged and stoned him.

8. Philip proclaimed Christ in Samaria. A magician offered money for the gift of the Spirit. Philip baptised an Ethiopian official.

9. Saul went to arrest the believers. Jesus said, "Why do you persecute me?" Saul was baptised and began preaching. Peter raised Dorcas.

10. Cornelius sent for Peter. The Lord said to Peter, "Do not call them unclean." Peter preached to the Gentiles and the Spirit fell.

11. Some in Jerusalem criticised Peter. He said, "The Spirit told me to go." Many in Antioch believed. Barnabas and Saul taught there.

12. Herod killed James and arrested Peter. The church prayed earnestly. An angel led Peter out of prison. An angel struck Herod down.

13. Paul and Barnabas proclaimed the word. Paul said, "God has sent a Saviour, Jesus, as he promised." The Jews stirred up persecution.

14. Many believed at Iconium. The crowd at Lystra wanted to worship Paul, then they stoned him. Paul and Barnabas returned to Antioch.

15. Some men taught circumcision for the Gentiles. Peter said, "God gave the Spirit with no distinction." Paul and Barnabas separated.

16. Paul took Timothy with him. We baptised Lydia in Philippi. Paul was imprisoned and there was an earthquake. The jailer was baptised.

17. They taught in Thessalonica and Berea. In Athens Paul said, "I proclaim the God who gives life to all. He will judge the world."

18. Paul taught in Corinth for a year and a half. He went to Ephesus with Priscilla and Aquila. Priscilla and Aquila taught Apollos.

19. Paul laid his hands on the disciples at Ephesus to receive the Holy Spirit. Demetrius, a silversmith, started a riot in the city.

20. We sailed to Troas. Paul raised Eutychus after he fell from the window. Paul encouraged the Ephesian elders to care for the flock.

21. Paul was warned not to go to Jerusalem. He said, "I am ready to die." We went there and saw James. Paul was arrested in the temple.

22. Paul said, "Jesus appeared to me and sent me to the Gentiles." The crowd threw dust. Paul told the tribune, "I am a Roman citizen."

23. Paul caused a dissension between the Pharisees and Sadducees. The Jews plotted to kill him. The tribune sent him to governor Felix.

24. Tertullus accused Paul before Felix. Paul said, "I simply went to worship in the temple." Felix kept Paul in prison for two years.

25. Festus arrived and summoned Paul. Paul said, "I appeal to Caesar." Festus brought Paul before King Agrippa to decide the charges.

26. Paul said, "I opposed the name of Jesus. He appeared to me and made me a witness." Agrippa said, "This man could have been freed."

27. We set sail for Rome. A storm struck and all hope was lost. Paul said, "Take heart, we must run aground." Everyone reached land.

28. On Malta Paul healed all who had diseases. We came to Rome. Paul lived under house arrest. He proclaimed the kingdom of God to all.

Romans

1. Paul, to the saints in Rome. I am eager to preach the gospel to you. The unrighteous have no excuse. God gave them up to their lusts.

2. In judging you condemn yourself. The doers of the law will be justified. Do you boast in the law but break it? A Jew is one inwardly.

3. The Jews were given the oracles of God. But no one is justified by the law. All have sinned and are justified through faith in Jesus.

4. Abraham was counted righteous by faith before he was circumcised. He is the father of all who believe. The promise depends on faith.

5. Therefore we rejoice in hope. While we were sinners, Christ died for us. As sin came through one man, so grace abounds through Christ.

6. We were baptised into Christ's death. So consider yourselves dead to sin and alive to God. Offer yourselves to God for righteousness.

7. You have died to the law. Is the law sin? No, sin produced death in me. I do not do what I want to do. My flesh serves the law of sin.

8. The law of the Spirit has set you free. We are children of God and co-heirs with Christ. Nothing can separate us from the love of God.

9. I grieve for my kinsmen. But not all Israel are Israel. God has mercy on whom he wills. Israel did not pursue righteousness by faith.

10. Everyone who calls on the Lord will be saved. How will they hear if no one preaches? Moses says of Israel, "I will make you jealous."

11. Even now there is a remnant of Israel. You Gentiles have been grafted into the tree. All Israel will be saved. Glory to God forever!

12. Present your bodies as a living sacrifice to God. We are one body in Christ. Love one another as brothers. Overcome evil with good.

13. Submit to authorities. Pay taxes to those due taxes. Owe nothing except love, which fulfils the law. Clothe yourselves with Christ.

14. Accept those who are weak in faith. Everything is clean but it is wrong to cause anyone to stumble. Whatever is not of faith is sin.

15. Each of us should build up our neighbours. Christ confirmed the promises given to the patriarchs. I hope to see you as I go to Spain.

16. I commend to you Phoebe. Greet Prisca, Aquila, Andronicus, Junia and Rufus. Avoid those who cause divisions. Glory to God forever!

1 Corinthians

1.   Paul, to the church in Corinth. Let there be no divisions. The cross is folly to those perishing, but to us it is the power of God.

2.   I knew nothing among you except Christ crucified. We speak the wisdom of God. Through the Spirit we know what God has freely given.

3.   You are still infants. One follows Paul, another Apollos. We are co-workers with God. Christ is the foundation. You are God's temple.

4.   Think of us as stewards of the mysteries of God. You are kings already? We are fools for Christ. I admonish you as my dear children.

5.   You boast about the sexual immorality among you. You should deliver that man to Satan. But I am not judging those outside the church.

6.   Do you take one another to court? Why not rather be wronged? Your body is not for sexual immorality, it is a temple of the Spirit.

7.   It is good to stay unmarried, but better to marry than to burn with lust. Each should live as God has called. I want you to be free.

8.   About food offered to idols: An idol is nothing. There is only one God. But if food makes my brother stumble I will never eat meat.

9. You are the seal of my apostleship. Do we not have the right to material support? But I made myself a servant to all for the gospel.

10. Do not desire evil as our fathers did. God will make you able to endure temptation. Flee from idolatry. Do all to the glory of God.

11. The head of a woman is her husband. I hear that some go hungry when you meet! With the bread and cup you proclaim the Lord's death.

12. Now there are various spiritual gifts, but one Spirit. If the whole body were an eye, how would it hear? You are the body of Christ.

13. Without love I am nothing. Love is patient, does not boast, endures all things. Tongues will cease, but faith, hope and love remain.

14. Tongues edifies the speaker, prophecy edifies the church. Each of you brings a hymn, a lesson or a tongue. Let all be done in order.

15. Christ was raised from the dead. If not then your faith is futile. But he is the firstfruits. At the trumpet we will all be changed.

16. Put aside an offering for the saints. I will come to you. The churches of Asia greet you. The grace of our Lord Jesus be with you.

2 Corinthians

1. Paul, to the church in Corinth. We share in Christ's sufferings and comfort. My yes is not no, but to spare you I did not visit you.

2. I wrote to you as I did in much anguish. You should forgive the one who caused you pain. Through us God spreads the aroma of Christ.

3. God has made us ministers of a new covenant. When anyone turns to the Lord, the veil is lifted. We are being transformed into glory.

4. God has given us the light of the glory of Christ. We have this treasure in clay jars. Through affliction we look to what is eternal.

5. What is mortal will be clothed with life. If anyone is in Christ, the new creation has come. We implore you, be reconciled to God!

6. Now is the day of salvation. We commend ourselves as servants. Do not be yoked with unbelievers. We are the temple of the living God.

7. I take great pride in you. I do not regret my letter, for godly grief produces repentance. Our boasts about you to Titus proved true.

8. The churches of Macedonia have given generously for the saints. See that you excel in this grace too. Titus was eager to go to you.

9. I boast to the Macedonians about the gift you promised. God loves a cheerful giver. Your generosity will overflow in thanksgivings.

10. Our weapons destroy arguments against God. What we say by letter we do in person. We only boast within the sphere God has given us.

11. I am jealous for you against these false apostles. I speak as a fool. Do they boast? I have greater labours, beatings and dangers.

12. I will boast of a man who saw paradise. I was given a thorn to keep me from pride. This is foolish! I will gladly be spent for you.

13. This will be my third visit. Christ is powerful among you. Test that you are in the faith. Be mature. The grace of God be with you.

Galatians

1. Paul, to the churches of Galatia. You are already turning to a different gospel! The gospel I preached came by revelation from Christ.

2. I went up to Jerusalem and saw the leaders. I opposed Cephas about circumcision. We are justified by faith in Christ and not by works.

3. Those who are of faith are blessed with Abraham. Christ has redeemed us from the curse of the law. In Christ you are all sons of God.

4. God sent his Son for us to receive adoption. How can you turn back to worthless principles? You, like Isaac, are children of promise.

5. Christ has set us free. Circumcision counts for nothing. Use your freedom to love one another. Walk by the Spirit and not the flesh.

6. Restore anyone caught in sin. Sow to the Spirit and reap eternal life. Let us not give up doing good. What counts is the new creation.

Ephesians

1. Paul, to the saints in Ephesus. Praise the God who predestined us for adoption in Christ. May you know the riches of his inheritance.

2. When we were dead in sin God made us alive with Christ. Gentiles are now fellow citizens. You are being built together into a temple.

3. I preach the mystery of Christ. The wisdom of God is made known through the church. I pray that you may know the depth of his love.

4. Therefore walk worthy of your calling. Christ gave each of us gifts to build up the body. Put off your old self and put on the new.

5. Walk in love as Christ loved us. Walk as children of light. Expose the darkness. Husbands, love your wives as Christ loved the church.

6. Children, obey your parents. Slaves, obey your masters. Put on the whole armour of God to stand against the devil. Peace and grace.

Philippians

1. Paul, to the saints in Philippi. I thank God for you. My imprisonment has advanced the gospel. To live is Christ and to die is gain.

2. Have the mind of Christ, who humbled himself even to a cross. Work out your salvation with trembling. I hope to send Timothy to you.

3. We put no confidence in the flesh. I count all things as loss compared to Christ. I press on towards the prize. Brothers, imitate me.

4. Rejoice in the Lord always! The peace of God will guard your hearts. I rejoice at your concern for me. My God will supply your needs.

Colossians

1. Paul, to the saints in Colossae. May you be filled with wisdom. The Son is the image of the invisible God. I make known the mystery.

2. Let no one deceive you. You were buried with Christ and also raised with him. Why do you follow rules that do not restrain the flesh?

3. Seek the things above. Your life is hidden with Christ in God. So put to death your worldliness. Do everything in the name of Jesus.

4. Devote yourselves to prayer. Let your speech be gracious. Tychicus will tell you our news. Aristarchus, Mark and Epaphras greet you.

1 Thessalonians

1. Paul, Silvanus and Timothy, to the Thessalonians. We give thanks for you. Our gospel came in power. Your faith is an example to all.

2. We shared the gospel with you and also our lives. You suffered like the churches in Judea. We tried to see you. Are you not our crown?

3. We sent Timothy to strengthen you. We warned you that persecution would come. We are encouraged by your faith. May you grow in love.

4. Live to please God. Avoid immorality. Love one another more and more. We do not grieve without hope, for the dead in Christ will rise.

5. The day of the Lord will come like a thief. Let us keep awake. Honour those who lead you. Do not quench the Spirit. Grace be with you.

2 Thessalonians

1. Paul, Silvanus and Timothy, to the Thessalonians. We boast of your faith through persecution. The Lord Jesus will appear in vengeance.

2. Do not be alarmed about the day of the Lord. First the lawless one will appear, whom Jesus will destroy. Hold fast to our traditions.

3. Finally, pray for us. The Lord will guard you against the evil one. Keep away from anyone who walks in idleness. The Lord be with you.

1 Timothy

1. Paul, to Timothy my son. Stay in Ephesus to correct false teachers. Christ came into the world to save sinners. Glory to God forever!

2. Let prayers be made for all those in authority. God wants everyone to come to the knowledge of the truth. Let women learn in silence.

3. An overseer must be respectable and manage his family well. Deacons must be dignified and not greedy. Godliness is a great mystery.

4. In later times some will depart from the faith. Have nothing to do with godless myths. Devote yourself to Scripture and to teaching.

5. Put widows over sixty on the list. Younger widows should marry. Elders who rule well are worthy of double honour. Keep yourself pure.

6. Those who contradict the teaching of Christ understand nothing. The love of money is a root of evil. Fight the good fight of faith.

2 Timothy

1. Paul, to Timothy my son. Fan into flame the gift of God. Share in suffering for the gospel. Hold to the standard of sound teaching.

2. No soldier gets entangled with civilian affairs. Present yourself to God as an approved worker. Cleanse yourself for honourable use.

3. In the last days, people will be proud and unholy. As for you, continue in what you have learned. All Scripture is inspired by God.

4. Preach the word in and out of season. I have finished my race. Come to me soon with Mark. Beware of Alexander. The Lord be with you.

Titus

1. Paul, a servant of God, to Titus. I left you in Crete to appoint elders. Deceivers must be silenced. To the impure nothing is pure.

2. Teach what is consistent with sound doctrine. Men are to be steadfast, women reverent. The grace of God trains us to live godly lives.

3. Show consideration to all. We were once slaves but God saved us. Believers should maintain good works. Everyone here sends greetings.

Philemon

1. Paul, a prisoner, to Philemon. I ask that you receive Onesimus back, not as a slave, but as a brother. Put his wrongs on my account.

Hebrews

1. In these last days God has spoken by his Son. Of the Son he says, "Let the angels worship him." And, "Your throne, O God, is forever."

2. We must pay closer attention. The author of salvation tasted death for everyone. He was made like us to make atonement for our sins.

3. Jesus has more honour than Moses. He is the Son over God's house. Therefore, "Do not harden your hearts as they did in the rebellion."

4. Let us fear lest anyone fails to reach the promised rest. The word of God judges the heart. So we boldly approach the throne of grace.

5. Every high priest from among men is subject to weakness. Christ is a high priest in the order of Melchizedek. You still need teaching.

6. Let us press on to maturity. It is impossible to restore those who fall away. The promise of God is a steadfast anchor for the soul.

7. Abraham gave a tithe to Melchizedek, who had no end. Our Lord became a priest through indestructible life. He is always able to save.

8. We have a high priest who ministers in the true tent. He mediates a better covenant. He says, "I will write my laws on their hearts."

9. The high priest enters the Most Holy Place once a year with blood. Christ entered the true holy place once for all by his own blood.

10. The law is but a shadow. Animal blood cannot take away sins. Christ offered one sacrifice forever. So let us hold fast to our hope.

11. Faith is the proof of hope. By faith the world was made. By faith Abraham obeyed. By faith Moses left Egypt. In faith some suffered.

12. Let us run the race, looking to Jesus. God is disciplining you as sons. See that no one falls short of grace. Let us worship in awe.

13. Let love continue. Marriage should be honoured. Let us bear the reproach Christ endured. Submit to your leaders. Grace be with you.

James

1. James, to the tribes. Many trials produce perseverance. Riches will fade. Every good gift comes from the Father. Be doers of the word.

2. If you show partiality to the rich you are committing sin. Act as those who are under the law of liberty. Faith without works is dead.

3. No one can tame the tongue. With it we bless our Father and with it we curse others. The wisdom from above is pure and peace-loving.

4. Your worldly desires cause conflict. Resist the devil, draw near to God. Who are you to judge your neighbour? You boast in arrogance.

5. You rich have fattened yourselves for slaughter. Brothers, be patient until the Lord comes. The prayer of faith will save the sick.

1 Peter

1. Peter, to the diaspora. God has given us new birth through Christ. The prophets told of this grace. So be holy in all your conduct.

2. You are being built up to be a royal priesthood. Submit to human authority. Live as servants of God. Follow Christ in his suffering.

3. Wives, submit to your husbands. Husbands, honour your wives. Repay evil with blessing. Christ suffered for sins to bring us to God.

4. Do not live for human desires but for the will of God. The end is near. Love each other deeply. Do not be surprised when trials come.

5. Elders should be examples to the flock. Clothe yourselves with humility. Resist the devil. God will strengthen you. Peace to you all.

2 Peter

1. Peter, to those of faith. God has given us great promises. So supplement faith with virtue and love. We were eyewitnesses of Christ.

2. False teachers will arise. If God did not spare angels, then he knows how to punish the unrighteous. They are slaves of corruption.

3. Scoffers will say, "Where is his return?" The Lord is not slow, but patient. Untaught people twist the Scriptures. Grow in Christ.

1 John

1. We have seen and proclaim to you the Word of life. God is light. If we walk in the light, the blood of Jesus cleanses us from all sin.

2. We know Christ if we keep his commands. Whoever loves his brother lives in the light. Do not love the world. Children, abide in him.

3. We are God's children. Those born of God do not sin. We should love one another. We know love because he laid down his life for us.

4. Any spirit that confesses Christ is of God. God is love. He sent his Son as a sacrifice for sins. If we live in love, God lives in us.

5. Anyone born of God overcomes the world. The Spirit, water and blood all testify. God gave us eternal life in his Son. Keep from idols.

2 John

1. The elder, to the elect lady. Let us love one another as the Father commands. Do not welcome false teachers. I hope to come to you.

3 John

1. The elder, to beloved Gaius. I was overjoyed to hear of your faithfulness. Diotrephes spreads false charges. I hope to see you soon.

Jude

1. Jude, to the elect. Ungodly people pervert grace into sensuality. They are judged as twice dead trees. Build yourselves up in faith.

Revelation

1. The revelation of Jesus Christ to John. A voice said, "Write to the churches." I saw one like a son of man, his face was like the sun.

2. "Ephesus, renew your first love. Smyrna, be faithful until death. Pergamum, some hold false teaching. Thyatira, you tolerate Jezebel."

3. "Sardis, you are not alive but dead. Philadelphia, you have endured in my word. Laodicea, you are lukewarm so I will spit you out."

4. I saw one seated on the throne in heaven. The four living creatures say, "Holy, holy, holy." The elders say, "You created all things."

5. A Lamb standing as though slain took the scroll with seven seals. The creatures, elders and myriad angels sang, "Worthy is the Lamb!"

6. The Lamb opened four seals and the horsemen went out to destroy. With the fifth seal I saw the martyrs. With the sixth the stars fell.

7. The 144,000 were sealed from the tribes. A multitude cried, "Salvation belongs to our God." An elder said, "God will wipe every tear."

8. With the seventh seal there was silence. I saw seven angels. Four angels blew their trumpets and a third of the earth was destroyed.

9. At the fifth trumpet, locusts from the pit tormented the earth. At the sixth trumpet, four angels killed a third of mankind with fire.

10. I saw an angel with a scroll. He cried out and seven thunders sounded. A voice said, "Eat the scroll." It was sweet and then bitter.

11. The two witnesses will prophesy until the beast kills them. At the seventh trumpet, loud voices said, "Our God shall reign forever."

12. A woman giving birth and a great dragon appeared. Michael and his angels fought the dragon. The dragon was thrown down to the earth.

13. I saw a beast rising out of the sea. It spoke blasphemy against God. Another beast rose and gave everyone a mark. Its number is 666.

14. I saw the Lamb in Zion with the 144,000. Angels said, "The hour of judgement has come." The earth was reaped with a sharp sickle.

15. I saw angels with seven plagues. Those who conquered sang, "Just are your ways, Lord!" The angels were given seven bowls of wrath.

16. The bowls of wrath were poured out. The seas turned to blood, darkness fell, the kings gathered at Armageddon and the earth quaked.

17. I saw a prostitute on a beast with seven heads and ten horns. An angel said, "The heads and horns are kings. The Lamb will conquer."

18. An angel cried, "Fallen, fallen is Babylon!" The kings and merchants will weep. An angel said, "The great city will be thrown down."

19. A multitude cried, "Hallelujah! The Lord reigns." The Word of God led the armies of heaven. The beast was cast into the lake of fire.

20. Satan was bound and the martyrs reigned with Christ for 1,000 years. Then Satan was cast into the lake of fire. The dead were judged.

21. I saw a new heaven and earth. A voice said, "God dwells with his people." An angel showed me the new Jerusalem. Its lamp is the Lamb.

22. The river of life flows from the throne of God. "Behold, I am coming soon. I am the beginning and the end." Amen. Come, Lord Jesus!